LLEWELLYN'S
CHAKRA ESSENTIALS SERIES

#1 • Root Chakra
JUNE 2023

#2 • Sacral Chakra
OCTOBER 2023

#3 • Solar Plexus Chakra
JUNE 2024

#4 • Heart Chakra
OCTOBER 2024

#5 • Throat Chakra
JUNE 2025

#6 • Third Eye Chakra
OCTOBER 2025

#7 • Crown Chakra
JUNE 2026

#8 • Out-of-Body Chakras
OCTOBER 2026

© Sweet Light Studio

Cyndi Dale is an internationally renowned author, speaker, and healer. She has written more than thirty books, including *Llewellyn's Complete Book of Chakras*; *Energy Healing for Trauma, Stress, and Chronic Illness*; *Kundalini*; and *The Complete Book of Chakra Healing*. Her year-long apprenticeship program through her company, Essential Energy, assists individuals in developing their natural intuitive and healing gifts. She also teaches in-depth classes via the Shift Network. Visit her at CyndiDale.com.

HEART CHAKRA

YOUR FOURTH ENERGY CENTER
SIMPLIFIED + APPLIED

EDITED BY
CYNDI DALE

LLEWELLYN
WOODBURY, MINNESOTA

FIRST EDITION
First Printing, 2024

Book design by Rebecca Zins
Cover design by Cassie Willett
Illustrations on pages 22 and 107–110 by Llewellyn Art Department

Llewellyn Publications is a registered trademark of Llewellyn Worldwide Ltd.

Library of Congress Cataloging-In-Publication Data (pending)

ISBN 978-0-7387-7329-2

Llewellyn Publications
A Division of Llewellyn Worldwide Ltd.
2143 Wooddale Drive
Woodbury, MN 55125-2989
www.llewellyn.com
Printed in the United States of America

CONTENTS

CONTENTS

PRACTICES

INTRODUCTION

You are a seeker. Your search may have included reading books indoors or spending time in nature, exploration or quiet reflection, romance or solitude—or all of these seemingly opposite approaches. Individually and collectively, we humans have journeyed into the great, the small, and everything in between looking for the ultimate grail: the meaning of life.

At some point, you probably guessed there wasn't a singular idea, religion, calling, or person that constituted the answer you were seeking. There were always more petals to unfold in your efforts to reveal the pistil, or center, of the flower of life. I'm going to suggest, however, that there is a chakra, or subtle energy center, that unfurls to reveal the essence of existence.

This chakra contains a special quality. My code phrase for it is "silent love."

This slightly paradoxical label joins other better-known names for the heart chakra. Named *anahata* in Sanskrit, the ancient language related to spiritual medicine, your fourth chakra is anchored in the center of your chest. Beating to the rhythm of your own uniqueness, the physical heart serves as the anchor for this amazing chakra that honors love and healing above all else.

Ironically, the Sanskrit meaning of anahata encapsulates what love is like: hard to figure out; a bit illogical; but oh, so worth it. The translation is "the unstruck sound."

Love is concrete, tangible, and active; it is also indescribable, ineffable, and elusive. Love really is like an unheard tone; you know it's there but can't exactly verbalize why. It is everywhere and nowhere. It embodies every human's principal motivation but is also the hardest goal to achieve.

Love is the reason a parent rises repeatedly in the middle of the night and a child cries over the gravesite of a parent. But when asked to define love, we find ourselves at a loss for words.

You can see why I call this the "silent love" chakra.

Chakras are dazzling, although basically they are nothing more (or less) than energy centers. Each manages specific frequencies that run a set of physical, psychological, and spiritual functions. Physically, your fourth chakra serves the bodily organs in your chest area. Psychologically, your heart chakra manifests your beliefs and feelings about love. Spiritually, anahata really does function as a silent love chakra. It helps you nobly receive, interpret, and disseminate intuitive information concerning healing and grace.

The bandwidth of frequencies related to your fourth chakra is usually perceived as green. This is a fitting hue, for what do we envision when we think of green but the way a tree's leaves reach for the sun, even when the rain is pelting? What an analogy for love: no matter what, we seek it. As the core chamber for love, our fourth chakra constantly transforms negative qualities such as greed and selfishness into truths like compassion and forgiveness. And when life is tough, this chakra renews us, promoting the release of the old and stale with the emergence of the innovative and bright.

What fun that this entire book is an exploration of your fourth chakra! It's also the fourth in an eight-book series called Llewellyn's Chakra Essentials.

This mini chakra series began with the first (root) chakra. Red as a flame, the root governs physical health and security needs. With our second book we moved upward from the hip region, the home of the first chakra, into the abdomen, the dwelling place of the second (sacral) chakra. Your emotions and creative potential circulate within this cauldron of bright orange. From the sacral chakra we journeyed into the solar plexus chakra. Sunshiny yellow, this third chakra manages mentality and guarantees success to all who illuminate its brilliance. Now, for our fourth step, we find ourselves in the heart chakra.

The next three books in the series will add even more knowledge to your in-body chakra education, and the eighth book will feature five out-of-body, or extraordinary, chakras. I'll speak about those again soon.

I know that most of us like order, but the universe also smiles upon inventiveness. You do not need to read any of the chakra books in numerical order. Each chakra is its own ecosphere and can be accessed as such.

All humans and most living beings are equipped with seven in-body chakras, which are based in the spine. These number from one to seven as they ascend from the coccyx to the top of the head. While every chakra busily performs its own sacred duties, they also continually interact with each other through the central nervous system, composed of the spine and the brain.

For context, we must thank the ancient Hindus for the term *chakra*, as it was first employed in the Indus Valley to signify "spinning wheels of light." That label is suitable as it depicts the fact that every chakra is in constant motion, linking our body, mind, and soul and accessing the various dimensions—hence the perception of a chakra as a whirling dervish or vortex. As well, the chakras' progression from the root of the spine to the top of the head is compared to a ladder reaching toward enlightenment. Each chakra movement—each step up—gets us closer to shining as the brilliant light we truly are.

The Hindus weren't the only ancient culture that embraced chakra concepts and bodies. The concept has existed across time and around the world among societies including the ancient Mayan, Aztec, Cherokee, Lakota, Hebrew, Berber, African Kemetic, and many Asian cultures. Nearly every civilization I've studied—and I've filled a 1,000-page book entirely with chakra research and depictions—has theorized the existence of chakra-like structures. These structures are nearly always described as vehicles that store the memories and programs that run us.

Central to all cross-cultural portrayals is the idea of chakras as energy centers. Energy is information that moves, and science asserts that everything is made of it. There are two types of energy, however. Very little—less than 1 percent—is physical, or measurable, while more than 99.9999-plus percent is subtle energy, also called spiritual, quantum, and psychic energy.[1] Chakras are essentially subtle energy centers, meaning they manage the invisible energy that ultimately determines what does and does not become apparent in 3D reality.

---

1   Ali Sundermier, "99.9999999% of Your Body Is Empty Space," Sciencealert, September 23, 2016, https://www.sciencealert.com/99-9999999-of-your-body-is-empty-space.

Your chakras aren't your only subtle energy structures. There are two other types, which I can best introduce by comparing them to your physical body's systems.

Three basic structures compose your physical body, which supervises your physical energies. These are the organs (like your liver and heart), channels (including the blood and lymph vessels), and fields, or oscillating vibrations (such as brain waves).

Comparably, you also have a subtle body that directs your subtle energies. Called the subtle energetic anatomy, it also consists of three basic structures. The primary organs are your chakras, the chief channels are your meridians and nadis, and the major fields of interest are your auric fields, which encircle you and are generated from the chakras.

Meridians stream through your connective tissue, moving subtle energies throughout the body. They are usually featured in traditional Chinese medicine and other Eastern healing modalities. The term *nadis* is Hindu in origin and labels the energy channels that are equivalent to your nerves. Both types of channels constantly exchange energy with the chakras.

Third in the subtle body trifecta are the auric fields, also called auric layers. Every chakra emanates its own field; together, they form the entire auric field, where every layer operates as a protective sheath for its companion chakra.

Based on the chakra's programming, the auric field determines which subtle (and sometimes physical) energies can enter or exit. In this book you'll learn all about the fourth auric field, which correlates to your fourth chakra.

Referenced every so often in this book, especially in part 1, will be a very special type of subtle energy that impacts both the subtle and physical anatomy. It is called *kundalini*. Kundalini is a divine energy that runs upward through the spine to cleanse your subtle and physical bodies and stairstep you toward enlightenment.

The word *kundalini* in Sanskrit means "coiled snake." Kundalini is pictured as a red serpent unfurling from the root chakra, located near the coccyx, to rise upward through the nadis and the seven in-body chakras. During its climb, the serpent, or red kundalini, can cause great upheaval, even catastrophe, as it triggers hidden physical and psychological issues, but it also offers the divine grace needed to heal these challenges and live in an awakened state. We'll look at kundalini in relation to the fourth chakra in part 1.

A WORD ABOUT THE
OUT-OF-BODY CHAKRAS

As promised, I'll now revisit the eighth book in the series, the one that will feature five out-of-body chakras. I work with a twelve-chakra system. Most systems feature only seven chakras, all positioned within the body. I employ twelve because I could perceive twelve chakras and auric fields when I was a child, seeing them with both my physical eyes and my inner eyes.

Then, beginning when I was in my twenties, I started studying with healers, shamans, intuitives, and gurus from around the world, including sites such as Venezuela, Peru, Costa Rica, and Morocco. Many of these experts also worked with more than seven chakras, and I've discovered that numerous ancient systems do the same. If you were educated about chakras in the West, however, you've probably been told that there are only seven. The truth is that spiritual medicine systems from around the world have depicted anywhere from three to dozens of chakras.

Since Llewellyn published my first book about the twelve-chakra system decades ago, it has taken off internationally. You will love interacting with your five extraordinary chakras. Knowledge of these chakras will add incredible depth to your understanding of yourself and the world. For instance, one of those higher chakras empowers mystical and interdimensional capabilities, and yet another enables the command of natural and supernatural forces.

Right now, however, we're all about heart.

A TOUR THROUGH THE BOOK

There are two sections to this book. Part 1, which I author, comprises three chapters covering the basics of the silent love chakra. These chapters mainly feature ancient Hindu knowledge, although other sources of enriching information are included. Throughout part 1 you will find practices to help you embrace the material.

In the first chapter, I cover anahata's overarching purpose, location, names, color, and sound. I also discuss the associated elements, breaths, lotus petals, affiliated god and goddess, and more.

Chapter 2 gets physical—literally; it's about biology. Rooted within its own spinal area, this chakra is also linked with an endocrine gland and other bodily areas. I'll describe the physical systems under its umbrella and the diseases that can strike if this chakra is out of alignment. Then, in chapter 3, we'll undertake yet another odyssey, this time into your fourth chakra's psychological and spiritual functions.

In part 2 I will hand you over to a band of wonderful new friends, each of whom will cover a specific topic and provide practices for improving your fourth chakra. One author will aid you in getting acquainted with your fourth chakra's spiritual allies, another will get you into heart-based yoga poses, and onward you'll travel until you've learned about fourth chakra guided meditations, vibrational remedies, stones, sounds, shapes, colors, and even recipes. Soon you'll be tuning in to the sounds of your silent love chakra, the source of life's mysteries and meaning.

PART 1

ESTABLISHING THE FOUNDATION
OF YOUR FOURTH CHAKRA KNOWLEDGE

• • • • • •

Inhale deeply into your chest. Exhale. For the next few moments, know that only love will enter and exit this space—deep love; real love; unconditional love. As you continue breathing deeply, imagine love illuminating your entire chest, the location of your heart chakra. What colors do you perceive emanating from this chakra? You might see or sense green—a lovely natural brilliant green—or maybe streams of pink or gold. Perhaps you've invested this area with other hues. Love is—and is reflected in—so many rainbow shades.

As you follow the flow of love throughout your chest, let that love intensify until it begins to stream throughout your body and beam into the environment. Whatever is not love is easily swept outside of you, and the universe will use this energy well, transmuting it for others' well-being.

You have just enabled a clearing and filling of your heart chakra. How do you feel right now? Before I release you from this process, I'd like to guide you through one more step.

Centering yourself again in the inner chamber of your heart chakra, within pure love, listen for the sound of love that is unique to you. You might intuitively hear or vibrationally sense a tone, a song, or a whisper of poetry. Perhaps you are aware only of silence, the "unstruck sound" of ana-hata referred to in its Sanskrit name.

Now complete this exercise with actual sound by what-ever verbal exclamation you are moved to utter: a bellow, chant, shout, hiss, or whoosh of air—whatever seems ful-filling and meaningful. Then settle back into your entire body and reenter the day.

Your silent love chakra is amazing, isn't it? So are you, frankly, when you live from this place of self, other, and divine love.

Your fourth chakra is the subtle energy center that gov-erns relationships, love, and healing, in addition to many bodily functions. Within its domain are organs including your heart, lungs, breasts, and other areas that are essen-tial to your health and well-being. Once you choose to fully cleanse and operate from your heart space, you'll find that the spiritual qualities invoking love—such as faith, hope, truth, appreciation, and gratitude—become your main-stays. At this point, your own essence of spirit can move right in, enabling you to fully embody all of this love for self and others.

Through the energy of this chakra, you'll learn how to make decisions beyond the bounds of karma, or unre-alized teachings about love. You'll learn to truly follow your heart and serve, without concern for the desires of the lower realms. Of course, that comes with a price, but it is so worth it. Within this silent love chakra, you confront the shadows of life—including lust, defiance, and anxiety—in such a way that, through devotion to compassion and honor, all is made well.

With anahata's awakening, you come to realize that within this energy center's void of silence, you will transcend any temptation toward violence. What counts here are matters of the heart and only the heart—matters that begin and end in love.

Welcome to part 1 of this book. Within it is a map serving the quest of learning about your fourth chakra. All three primary levels of your heart chakra's powers are featured: physical, psychological, and spiritual.

Each of the three chapters in this section relates to a vital area of fourth chakra knowledge. In the first chapter I'll shine a light on the knowledge we have inherited from Hindu culture, also showcasing other facets of chakra information from more contemporary sources. In chapter 2 I'll explore the physical nature of your heart chakra. In chapter 3 I'll showcase the brilliance of this chakra's psychological and spiritual qualities. In the end, the unheard sound of love will sing as loudly as it needs to so you can know yourself as love.

1

FUNDAMENTALS

Think about how much of your life is devoted to heart. I don't mean only the physical heart, though we're reminded of the importance of that organ every time we notice it beating. I mean heart as in the awareness and search for love, healing, and transformation—the ability to embrace and offer all good things.

Greet your heart chakra, the subtle energy center that manages so many levels of your physical, psychological, and spiritual well-being.

Within this energy center are the ideas and programs that create your openness to relationships—with self, others, and whatever you may call the Spirit. I've found most individuals believe that the purpose of life is relationship, and the heart chakra would certainly testify to that matter. One vitally important reason to thoroughly comprehend the nature of your silent love chakra is that it is key to the simplest of joys. Whatever your heart's desires are, in some way they will each be based in relationship and love.

In this chapter I'll first treat you to a true story about the power of the heart chakra. Several mini sections will then help you mine the treasures of this all-powerful chakra. Much of the information is based on Hindu ideals and reflections about the fourth chakra. This ancient wisdom spans thousands of years of expertise and insights. Especially in matters of the heart, it is inspirational to receive a traditional education from the elders. Every so often, I'll offer perspectives that are more modern. These reflections will guarantee that the data I present can find a secure home in your everyday life.

Any teaching is made more meaningful through related practices, so interspersed with the information in these chapters will be exercises for you that create a clear and thoughtful pathway into and through your fourth chakra.

Let's now enter the portal of love.

THE ESSENCE OF YOUR FOURTH CHAKRA

Marvin was frequently called "Marvel" by his friends because everything in his life seemed magical.

A broad-shouldered Black American, Marvin had been a football star in college before being sidelined by a severe muscle pull. That didn't stop him, though. He continued as an assistant coach while putting himself through grad school. Soon thereafter, he married his college sweetheart, with whom he shared two children. Over time, he rose to the position of vice president at a Fortune 500 company.

Then he came to see me.

Marvin—Marvel, as he introduced himself—wouldn't initially describe the true nature of his problems, except to share that he had a slight heart arrhythmia. Physiologically, arrhythmia presents as an uneven heartbeat, which has several possible medical causes. In the subtle energy realm, arrhythmias often present because the heart is beating for two "masters." A person might be bonded with two different and competing loves and not know what to do.

When I brought up that potential, Marvel was tight-lipped. He asked me to perform my intuitive job and share what came to me.

Bottom line: I perceived two areas of his life that were pulling Marvel's heart—or heart chakra—in different directions. He loved his wife, but it appeared to me intuitively that he was also in love with someone else—a man. As if that wasn't stressful enough, his heart was also pulled by another issue. He was good at his job and proud of his success, but he longed to return to football.

Marvel asked me how I could know these things about him. I told him that I saw intuitive images and received messages psychically from what I believed were his guides, which is my gift. More importantly, I believed that his heart had spoken to me directly through my mystical senses.

Marvel and I spent several sessions together. As we worked through the cultural and family issues that insisted he be straight rather than gay and earn a living in a corporate rather than athletic career, his heart started to beat less erratically. His cardiologist had advised they wait and see, so he hadn't yet started any medical treatment. While working with me, Marvel also saw his therapist and participated in couples counseling with his wife, whom I'll call Alice.

Marvel started to consider—and, equally important, act upon—some life-changing decisions with the benefit of this support. After a few months, he decided to complete a master's degree in sports training and coaching while working his corporate job. He then made a clean break.

"I'm going to return to the field," he announced to me, although not as a player; rather, he would serve as a coach. He also initiated a separation from his wife.

For her part, Alice adored Marvel. After he shared what he needed to do, she came to a session with him to see me. She admitted that she had often wondered about his sexual identity, and she loved him enough to support him no matter what.

After two years of living apart, the two completed a supportive divorce. Marvel finished his education while coaching at a junior college. He entered a relationship with a man. And his heart rhythm completely stabilized. He was eventually offered an even better coaching position. Marvel credits his healthy heart with coming clean in relationship with himself first and foremost.

The heart chakra knows what is best for us—if we only have the eyes to see and the ears to hear.

OVERARCHING PURPOSE

Anahata is the energy center of unconditional love and right relationship, initiating healing when needed. In short, it is the temple of self-honesty and compassion.

IT'S ALL IN THE NAME: TERMS FOR THE FOURTH CHAKRA

As you learned in the introduction, *anahata* can be translated as "unstruck sound." It can also mean "unhurt" and "unbeaten."

Another name for the anahata found in the Upanishads, ancient Hindu texts written in Sanskrit, is dwadashara chakra.

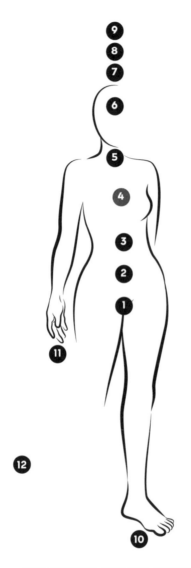

THE TWELVE-CHAKRA SYSTEM

LOCATION OF THE FOURTH CHAKRA

Your fourth chakra is found between your breasts. It is aligned with the sushumna nadi, which is basically the spine. This nadi is also considered to be the source of the heart chakra's sound. The fourth chakra divides the body into lower and upper hemispheres, with the centers beneath the heart chakra representing the more primitive forms of consciousness, such as those involved with the physical world and pleasure seeking. The higher chakras, those above anahata, are thought to interact with the realms devoted to spiritual consciousness.

COLOR OF THE FOURTH CHAKRA

Every chakra vibrates at its own set of frequencies. You could say that a chakra is a bandwidth composed of a specific spectrum of colors and range of sounds. You'll learn all about the sound (and silence) of your silent love chakra in the next section; right now, we'll jump into the fourth chakra's coloration.

The fourth chakra usually governs energies in the green spectrum. Green reflects the energy of healing and renewal, inviting refreshment, restfulness, and security. Green also helps balance the two hemispheres of the brain, evening out the mind when it's playing teeter-totter. Notably, green is formed from two other colors. Its blue tones are soothing and the yellow tones are invigorating. It's a great hybrid for stimulating nerves and glands and prompting physical activity while also allowing for relaxation if we get too stressed.

Of course, there are various shades of green. Light greens are sprinkled with sunlight and cheer; dark greens grant growth and composure. As with anything in life, the different hues of green can also invoke negative reactions. A muddy green can indicate sluggish thinking or a depressive state of mind, while a gray to brackish green can be associated with envy, materialism, and greed. Be flexible with your good greens to enjoy the most out of your love life—and that includes your partnerships with self, others, and the Divine.

The heart chakra is also described by a secondary color: pink. Pink is a soothing color and indicates that a person's heart is serving higher ends. Occasionally I meet someone whose heart chakra glimmers with gold. I find that indicates a person devoted to selfless service.

You'll have fun with various colors that can bolster your fourth chakra in chapter 12.

SOUND OF THE FOURTH CHAKRA

According to Hindu teachings—and the teachings of many ancient cultures, actually—every chakra resonates with its own unique tone. Like a bell, this sound reflects the truth of a chakra, and when stimulated it can enable balancing and cleansing.

These tones are called *bijas* (seed sounds). Other terms for these chakra harmonics are *bija mantras* (master sounds). When repeated aloud or internally, a mantra can bring about a meditative state. Regarding your fourth chakra, you can employ its sacred sound for all kinds of uplifting purposes. You'll receive tips on various sound practices in chapter 11.

In modern spiritual circles, the heart chakra has been paired with the F note. It is the fourth step of a sequence that starts with a C in the first chakra, moves to D in the second chakra, and strikes an E in the third chakra.

From a traditional Hindu perspective, the bija is *Yam*. In this love chakra, the sound is pronounced "yum" if you are chanting it.

Each seed syllable is associated with a god and goddess in the Hindu pantheon. In the *bindu* (dot) above the syllable *Yam*, which is dark gray in color, resides the god Ishana Rudra Shiva, also called Isvara. The goddess related to this sound and the fourth chakra is Kakini Shakti. You will read about both these deities soon.

The relationship of sound to the silent love chakra is more complicated and lovely than can be explained through understanding the bija. Remember that anahata means "unstruck sound," among other "un" terms. One of the reasons for these "un" names is that as the various forms of prana, or vital breath, flow through the sushumna—the central energy channel along the spine—into the third chakra, the seed sounds of the alphabet automatically appear in the fourth chakra. These sounds vary depending on the shape and breadth of the different nadis. The more powerful the pressure of the air on the chakra, the more pronounced the seed sound. The important thing to note is that the sounds of these letters are generated without external friction, the way sound waves are usually created, hence the term "unstruck sound."

PRACTICE

MANTRA TO CREATE PEACE INSTEAD OF FEAR

The heart is particularly responsive to fear. When we're scared, our heartbeat flutters and we get stuck in negative thinking. In such a state, it's easy to worry about the future and become entrenched in past mistakes.

The following mantra can be particularly helpful in releasing fear and establishing a sense of peace. You can repeat it as often as needed aloud or silently.

Om shante shante sarvarishta nashini swaha
(pronounced *Om SHANT-tay SHANT-tay*
sar-VAR-ish-ta na-SHIN-ee SWA-ah)

This ancient, mystical, and multileveled mantra can be interpreted this way:

O Sacred One, toward peace, toward peace.
You are the means of accomplishing the removal
of sufferings. This is the prayer we offer.

SOUND CARRIER

All chakras are linked to a being that carries the sound of that chakra. The unique carrier of *Yam* is the black antelope or gazelle, which symbolizes the lightness of physical substance.

An incredibly swift animal, the black antelope serves the air element and Purusha, the Supreme Being, who will be discussed later in this chapter in relation to the yantra, or overarching chakra symbol.

Ruminate on the qualities of this animal. An antelope is shy and graceful, implying a spirituality that avoids the ego-centered self. It is elegant and slender, with small cloven hooves and powerful hindquarters. It is protective, perceptive, and mindful. Its black color speaks to the nature of universal mysteries and reminds us that there is always more to life and love than we can easily see at first glance.

LOTUS PETALS AND APPEARANCE

Lotus petals are beautiful stylizations used to depict all of the in-body chakras. What makes them fascinating is that every chakra has a different number and color of petals.

Though lotus petals are aesthetically beautiful, they also hold deeper meaning. From a subtle energy point of view, the petals describe the chakra's swirling motion.

Every chakra takes in, processes, and emanates subtle energies that match its band of frequencies. It also interacts with the physical energies that bubble within this same frequency spectrum. That means that a chakra is affected by the vibrational movements and data related to the physical organs, fluids, sound waves, and electromagnetic frequency (EMF) activity in its localized area. A chakra is also affected by the subtle energies swirling inside and outside a being. If you were to suddenly stop the whirling, radiating energies of a chakra, you would perceive an image of a vortex with several outstretching arms of EMF and sound. These extensions would look like the petals of a lotus flower.

By focusing on the entire lotus and the specific petals of a particular chakra, you absorb the spiritual qualities of that chakra. That is a fitting outcome because in India the lotus represents spiritual life. These hardy flowers are anchored in muddy water, yet their blossoms reach toward the sun. The cloudiness at the base cannot hide the beauty above.

In a way, this is the story of life. No matter where we come from, no matter what in our background may seem muddy and murky, goodness can emerge. The life spring of water, which the Hindus compare to maya (the illusion of life), invites us to struggle upward to arrive at—and share— our true essence. Nothing could be more core to the true self and the ultimate function of the world than to reveal love and only love.

The lotus of anahata showcases twelve vermilion petals. Upon each is inscribed a syllable: these are kam, kham, gam, gham, ngam, cham, chham, jam, jham, nyam, ttam, and ttham. These syllables match the *vrittis* (thoughts) that surface from the mind of lust, fraud, indecision, repentance, hope, anxiety, longing, impartiality, arrogance, incompetence, discrimination, and defiance. Through the struggles of life and relationship, we are invited to move through the whirlpool of negative qualities and emerge triumphant— and clear about what is most vital.

FOURTH CHAKRA SYMBOLS: THE YANTRA

A yantra is a geometric design that is a sort of diagram of subtle energetics. Yantras have been used for over 13,000 years in Indian culture to assist with meditation.

Usually a yantra represents a specific god or goddess. The idea is that when you focus on a yantra, whether it is shown visually on paper or on your inner mind screen, you are linked with the deity. In turn, the deity can send you healing and guidance. A yantra can also be adopted to hold a specific task or promise in mind. Some of those vows might be conscious. Others could have been contracted by your soul before you were born to bolster your commitment to achieving a life purpose or expressing your true self.

Within the fourth chakra yantra, or chakra symbol, the smoky gray lotus flower with twelve petals contains a *shaktona*, a symbol of masculine and feminine unification. It consists of overlapping, intersecting triangles that create a hexagram. The triangle facing upward symbolizes Shiva, one of the main deities of Hinduism. The triangle pointing downward is Shakti, who is a great goddess. In Hinduism, gods and goddesses appear in many forms. The specifics of the fourth chakra yantra point to Purusha (a name for the Supreme Being) and Prakriti (the mother of matter). The deity of this region is Vayu, who is the color of smoke and has four arms. He holds an *angkusha,* or goad (a stick used to herd animals), and rides an antelope, which is this chakra's sound carrier.

Linked to this chakra is the bhana lingam, more completely described in this chapter's granthi section. It is an energetic knot that must be untied to enable the rise of the kundalini, the divine life energy.

GROSS ELEMENT

According to many religions, matter is composed of different elements. In Eastern religions, it is thought that there are four basic elements: earth, water, fire, and wind (or air). In some systems there exists a fifth element: space. The element of the fourth chakra is air.

The invisible element of air is a powerful force that affects the world within and around us. It is traditionally described as having qualities including lightness, movement, and clarity. I often ascribe mental activity to it, as air can carry, transfer, and release ideas. It is more than fitting that air is linked to the silent love chakra, as it is often related to the breath, which enters through the lungs, one of several organs found in the heart chakra area. Air is also considered a suitable heart chakra element in that often anahata is labeled the seat of the soul. I personally find this to be both poetic and practical; where would a person's soul be located other than the home of love?

Color of the Gross Element

As I noted earlier, the gross or major element of the fourth chakra is air. There are several colors (or lack thereof) associated with the air element. These are colorless, gray, and tepid green.

Think of how elusive air is. Sometimes it is still; at other times it is wildly violent. This makes it hard to portray it as a single color, which is why the hues describing it range from no color to a silver or cloudy gray to almost green.

PREDOMINANT SENSE AND SENSE ORGAN

Every in-body chakra is associated with a sense and a sensory organ. This information, along with knowledge of an action organ (described in the next section), comes from *The Serpent Power* by Sir John Woodroffe.[2] This groundbreaking book officially brought chakras to the Western world in the early twentieth century and is based on several ancient Hindu texts.

In his book, Woodroffe explains that in the Eastern world, the senses are considered gateways for worldly experiences. A sense (*indriya*) is partnered with a sense organ (*jnanendriya*) to support the physical body, but those organs

---

2   Arthur Avalon (pseudonym for John Woodroffe), *The Serpent Power* (Madras: Ganesh & Co.: 1950), a803206.us.archive.org/3/items /TheSerpentPowerByArthurAvalon/The%20Serpent%20Power %20by%20Arthur%20Avalon.pdf.

are actually considered an instrument for empowering the mind. A yogi, for instance, can pick up on a sense without using the sense organ.

The association of a sense and sense organ with subtle activity doesn't mean that the physical apparatus is any less important. Having made this statement, the sense associated with anahata is touch, and the sense organ is the skin.

Think about how vital touch is to our well-being. Infants who aren't touched enough or in a loving enough way can develop a failure to thrive and quite literally starve. That is how important touch is to the body and the soul.

Of course, there is healthy touch and touch that isn't healthy. Unhealthy touch is the type we tell our children to be worried about. If you have been victimized at any point in your life by unsavory touch, such as what occurs with physical abuse, it can be hard to know when you want to be touched and when you don't or what to do if someone is hurting or threatening you. The heart chakra is very much the center of love, and its job of holding the soul can illuminate your ability to distinguish between desired and undesired touch.

Some individuals are willing to put up with bad-feeling touch because they long for any sort of connection. Again, the heart knows that you always deserve love and only love, and it will help you say no or yes in the right context.

ACTION ORGAN

Every in-body chakra is related to an action organ, a region in the body that invites physical energy into the chakra and fills it with vim and vigor. The action organ for your fourth chakra is the sexual organs.

As per John Woodroffe, the action organ (*karmendriya*) of the heart chakra is your genitalia. It would be more logical to suppose that the action organ related to the chest area are your hands, as they extend from the heart chakra, or the lungs, which directly relate to the oxygenation of your cardiovascular system. Action organs, however, must be understood in relation to the senses. As Woodroffe explains it, an organ of action is a reaction to a sensation. As per the heart chakra, the genitals respond to our need to procreate, which could be seen as one of the heart's desires that is certainly related to touch and the skin.

Think of the cervix. Both the heart and the cervix mirror openness and vulnerability. The testes are unprotected by the skeletal system, so when used in the sexual act, they are open and exposed. In fact, all the acts of coupling, no matter the gender or sexual identity of the partners, is about giving and receiving intimacy through contact. The unifying power of love is meant to be enjoyed as often as possible outside of the ego's strictures, inviting warmth and connection. Overall, the sexual organs diffuse life. If we join this life-giving potentiality with the love of the heart, even when we're not engaged in the activity of sex, we'll be creating more love for self and others.

VITAL BREATH

In Hinduism the life force is called prana. Prana is a very real yet ethereal energy that moves through all living beings. It assures vibration, activity, and our very lives. It is also called spirit breath, breath of life, and the vital principle. The most obvious manifestation of prana is the breath, although prana is considered a subtle energy.

Many of the chakras are also associated with a particular form of vital winds. These are called *vayus*, and there are five in number. All five magical winds wind together to form patterns of energetic flow to release blockages, invigorate the chakras, feed the sushumna/spine, and expand your soul awareness. Interestingly, the wind of your anahata is prana, the most vital of all life forces. When prana vayu is imbalanced, you might develop anxiety, low energy, poor immune function, breathing irregularities, poor circulation, and more. Know that whenever you take a deep and clear inhalation, you fill your entire subtle and physical body with prana, with an extra special amount delivered to your heart chakra. Exhalations release toxins of all levels for your entire self and your heart chakra in particular.

ATTRIBUTE

An attribute is a quality, and every in-body chakra is associated with a specific quality that relates to its sound carrier. Your special sonic being for your heart chakra is the black antelope, which carries the attribute of restlessness.

We don't tend to think of restlessness as a positive characteristic, but it is an important trait. When we're in a state of disquiet, we are ready to act, to try new things. Restlessness also enables us to be aware of dangers and opportunities so we can shift with the nimbleness and speed of the antelope. Be grateful for the times when you are restless in your heart chakra, and follow that inclination.

RULING GODDESS

Ruling the heart chakra is the Kakini Shakti. With her rose-colored skin and sky blue sari, she is seated upon a pink lotus and holds a sword, shield, skull, and trident. As the doorkeeper of your silent love chakra, she moves like air throughout the body, infusing you with love. She is also the goddess of spiritual music, poetry, and heart, all the sounds (and unsounds) of love, enabling your fourth chakra to function as a seed that continually begets the entire tree of self.

RULING GOD

Anahata's associated god is Ishana Rudra Shiva, sometimes called Isvara. Peaceful and benevolent, he has camphor blue skin and holds a trident in his right hand and a drum in his left. His flowing hair is symbolic of the Ganges River, a stream of self-knowledge that pronounces "I am that." The snakes coiled around his body represent the passions, which he has tamed. To his devotees he bestows wisdom and abundance, and we could all use more of both.

RULING PLANET

We've spoken of the heart chakra as related to the genitalia and to love, so of course it is considered to be ruled by Venus. As the planet of love, pleasure, and beauty, Venus is so fitting for the heart's endeavors.

GRANTHI (KNOT) AND LINGA

The heart chakra is home to two very important energetic structures. The first is a granthi and the second is a linga, a term interchangeable with lingam.

The term *granthi* means "knot" and "doubt" in Sanskrit. In relationship to anahata—and a yogi devoted to the rising of kundalini and the process of enlightenment—a granthi is a challenging knot or puzzle that must be untied. Granthis are psychic knots that, when unwound, enable the free flow of prana and the rising of the soul's awareness in the body.

There are three granthis related to the chakras: the brahma granthi, located in the first chakra; the rudra granthi, linked with the sixth chakra; and the vishnu granthi, found in the fourth chakra.

The vishnu granthi is associated with the *uddiyana bandha* (abdominal valve) in the body and is most frequently linked with the heart chakra, although it is sometimes perceived as being between manipura (the third chakra) and anahata. Vishnu is the god of preservation, and he asks us to untie this knot to open *karuna* (compassion). In doing so we accept the responsibility of serving others with devotion and love while releasing the desire to focus on our self-identity. This granthi is related to the bhana lingam, around which the kundalini is wound three and a half times.

A *lingam* is a sign, seal, or mark that generally represents the Hindu god Shiva. It is inscribed as a devotional image in many Hindu temples, where it is often represented within a vertical disc-shaped platform. Its counterpart is a horizontal platform that symbolizes the yoni, or feminine counterpart. In general, a lingam—in a chakra or as a prayer object—is the outward symbol of primordial matter. In relation to the yoni, these conjoined masculine and feminine complements create unity consciousness. The lingam often appears in Hindu culture in the form of a phallus, emphasizing its masculine properties.

Anahata's bindu, the dot above the chakra seed syllable, coincides with the tip of the silent love chakra's linga. It isn't considered to be pierced by the sushumna but is often seen as an empty space around a circle.

There are three granthis in the energetic body. These are knots that must be unwound for the kundalini to ascend. They are in the forms of lingas or lingams, which are symbols of Shiva. The heart chakra is associated with the vishnu lingam or granthi, which is also sometimes called the bhana lingam. It is associated with its own form of Rudra Shiva or Sadashiva, meaning "eternal benefactor." He is also known as the Shabda Brahma or the eternal logos, or word. As such, he is also called Omkara: the combination of the three gunas of sattva, rajas, and tamas, which are symbolized by the trident he holds.

A *guna* is a quality or property. These three gunas are represented by the universal AUM (or OM). The vishnu lingam is the symbol of the subtle work through which we perceive the universal life principle and is often seen as red or gold in color.

It is critically important to unwind the vishnu granthi repressing the kundalini from flowing upward, as the heart chakra is the pivot point between the three lower and more worldly chakras and the three higher, more spiritual chakras. Once freed for her climb, this divine snake enhances our own personal signature, which is easiest to sense in our heart space. As a result, the lower chakras can blossom even more beautifully and we can sing more wondrously our own song into and through the higher chakras.

RELATED AURIC FIELD

The auric field for the fourth chakra is the fourth auric field.

In the twelve-chakra system, the fourth auric field is found about a foot from the skin. It is just outside the third auric field, which is atop the second auric layer. The first auric field lies within the skin and outward to about an inch and a half around the entire body.

The fourth auric field is programmed by the ideas within your fourth chakra, which are a library of ancestral experiences. Embedded in anahata are also imprints from your own childhood, your family of origin, and experiences from your life. Also stored are cultural and societal norms and your ideas about them. Many fourth auric field programs are negative, which means they don't match your spiritual ideas, but they can be transformed by healing the fourth chakra.

We can often detect relationship ills in this auric field that fall within the fourth chakra's jurisdiction. The most harmful usually relate to broken and abusive relationships, which often leave us feeling unlovable. You'll be able to employ many of the practices in this book to heal those war wounds.

THE ANAHATA'S SECONDARY CHAKRA: THE CELESTIAL WISHING TREE

There is a beautiful chakra often associated with the heart chakra. It is typically called the *surya* or *hrit* chakra, but my favorite term for it is the celestial wishing tree.

While it is often affiliated with the fourth chakra, it is also associated with the solar plexus chakra because it's found just below the heart and in the left side of the solar plexus. However, I believe this chakra is meant to be moved to the very center of your heart chakra so it can be accessed for its true purpose: to enable your heart's desires. Because of this, following this section I include a practice to enable that transference.

In a nutshell, your celestial wishing tree is often considered the spiritual heart, which is in contrast to the body's physical heart.

The hrit has its own lotus, called the *anandakanda*, which means "root" or "bulb of bliss." It has eight petals, each

41

of which represents an emotion: dullness, anger, evil, joy, movement, sexuality, charity, and holiness. These petals, which are gold, white, or red, also represent eight super-powers. *Hrit* means "heart," which is fitting, as this chakra is found within the chitrini nadi in the vertebral column.

There are three layers or interdependent nadis within the sushumna. The outer layer, called the vajra nadi, is the dense physical layer. Immediately below it is the chitrini nadi, which rises from the first to the sixth chakras. It is extraordinarily fine, depicted as stain free, and thought to be untouched by the world's impurities. And if you're curious, the core or innermost nadi is the brahma nadi. It is composed of luminous spiritual energy. The celestial wishing tree itself faces downward and could be considered as composing the lower part of anahata.

This chakra is also called the *hridaya* chakra, meaning "he who dwells in the heart" and considered the point where energy and matter meet to emanate the aroma of bliss. When shown as mainly golden in color, it could be called the *surya* (sun) chakra. It is in this depiction that it is most often linked to the solar plexus chakra. The argument for this belief is that this chakra provides heat to the third chakra.

There are three regions in the hrit. First is a vermilion sun region, within which is a white moon. Inside the moon is a deep-red fire region, and inside this is the *kalpataru*, a red wish-granting tree. This enchanting tree represents our ability to manifest our deepest soul's desires. The tree, which was given us from the Heaven of Indra, is depicted with an altar in front of it and a white bird in its branches. Often a petitioner is shown kneeling at the altar, creating wishes that the bird will carry to the heavens for a deity to grant. The eight petals play a role in the tree's enchantment; whether they are gold or white, we wish upon the petals. It is said that this tree bestows even more upon adepts than they desire.

In Tibetan Buddhism, the celestial wishing tree chakra is affiliated with essences, also called drops, that have their origins in the heart chakra. These dissolve at death to carry our consciousness to our next lives. The wishing tree functions as its own chakra and is depicted as white and circular, with eight downward-pointing petals. Its seed syllable is *Hum*. In the Tantric Tibetan tradition, this chakra is located between the heart and the throat chakras.

No matter how you perceive your celestial wishing tree, it's time to create a dream within it.

PRACTICE

MOVING YOUR CELESTIAL WISHING TREE INTO YOUR HEART CHAKRA

The celestial wishing tree is usually found underneath the left side of your rib cage and at the top of the solar plexus chakra. It is ideal to bring this dream-body into the center of your heart chakra so your deepest heart's desires can manifest.

» To do this, take a few deep breaths and settle yourself. Feel your feet on the ground. Relax your shoulders and arms so you can enjoy this process.

» Rest one of your hands on the left side of your solar plexus. You'll be in contact with the lower left ribs and stomach region of your body. Press lightly down into this area and allow yourself to picture the celestial wishing tree as it was described in the previous section. Basically, you will envision a chakra with an eight-petaled lotus. Focus on creating the image of the enchanted tree with a white bird in it. An altar is placed before the tree, and a petitioner is kneeling at the altar.

» You will now imagine yourself as the petitioner in this chakra.

» Your first wish, which you make when focused upon the eight petals, is for Indra to move the chakra from its current place to the very middle of your heart chakra. Move your hand from its position on your solar plexus to the center of your heart chakra and know that this chakra is becoming affixed in anahata's core with beams of love.

» From this position, and still playing the role of the prayerful one, create a desire. Bring it forward from the depths of your heart and embrace the full wonder of your aspiration. This ambition was forged in the stars by your soul and longs to be born. Then envision yourself sending this bidding to the waiting wings of the white bird, which first catches your wish and then kisses you with its beak before flying away, carrying your hope to Indra, who will honor your request.

» When the bird returns to its bough, know that it has delivered your dream. Thank this special carrier and take a few deep breaths. Your request is being tendered. Breathe deeply again in and through your heart chakra. Remain grounded—attuned to the ground and your entire body—and return to your everyday life when you're ready.

COSMIC PLANE

There is one more historical detail to note about your fourth chakra. The in-body chakras are often associated with realms of existence that lie below the first chakra. These planes are called *lokas*, and they look like luminous spheres. Lokas are essentially cosmic realms, and the one linked to the fourth chakra is called the mahar loka realm. This is a place of balance that is home to sages and enlightened beings.

SUMMARY

So much of love and life is about the heart, and the longing for love, relationships, and healing is encompassed in your heart chakra. Green in color, anahata houses the air element, which is often considered clear in coloration and manages all the organs and body parts in your chest area as well as the cardiac plexus in the spine.

With the genitalia serving as the action organ, it's little wonder the sense is touch and the sense organ is the skin. Represented as a lotus flower with twelve smoky gray petals, its yantra is a *shaktona*, which integrates male and female energies. The sound *Yam*, carried by the black antelope, can be chanted to access the god Ishana Rudra Shiva and the goddess Kakini Shakti. And if you untie the granthi and lingam associated with the heart chakra, upward climbs your kundalini, ready to bestow love through the struck and unstruck sounds of life.

Now that you've learned the foundational components of your heart chakra, let's move onward to the physicality of this silent love chakra.

2

THE PHYSICAL SIDE

Although we mainly consist of subtle energy, our physicality is equally important to acknowledge. This is exceptionally true of the fourth chakra as we can function well only if the areas of the body that are associated with it are hale and healthy.

We could not survive without our essential organ, the heart. As the center of cardiovascular activity, it is also essential in respiration and the movement of blood throughout the system, amongst other tasks. In this deep dive into the physiology of your silent love chakra, consider making a vow such as this one to yourself:

I promise to support my fourth chakra
so I might be healthy in all ways.

OVERVIEW OF THE FOURTH
CHAKRA'S PHYSICAL REACH

Your fourth chakra is rooted in your chest area, including the front and back of the chest.

This chakra corresponds to the cardiac plexus, a collection of nerves at the base of the heart. Also linked to this plexus is the epicardium, the membrane forming the innermost layer of the pericardium and the outer surface of the heart. It relates to numerous cardiac branches that come off the vagus nerve—a core regulator of most organic processes in the body—as well as several sympathetic nerve trunks and other ganglia. The vagus nerve extends all the way from the brain stem into the abdomen and manages everything from the immune system to emotions.

Like every other chakra, the fourth has a major endocrine gland, and in this case, that organ is the heart itself. I like to compare the heart to the center of your own universe. Commit to heart health and you become a devotee of your entire body.

AREAS OF THE BODY MANAGED

Anahata manages dozens of duties, especially those related to your cardiovascular and respiratory functions. Rooted in the cardiac plexus, anahata manages the heart, circulatory system, blood, lungs, rib cage, breasts, shoulders, arms, hands, and, along with other chakras, the diaphragm and esophagus. It is also linked with your thymus, a gland that plays an important role in your immune system. Given its many tasks within your cardiovascular and breathing systems, it is the main chakra on the biological level for bringing fresh, oxygenated blood into the body.

ASSOCIATED GLAND:
THE HEART

There are two philosophies about which gland is most closely associated with anahata: one group believes the heart is its endocrine gland, while the other votes for the thymus. Most systems locate the ruler of this chakra in the heart, as do I. The interrelationship between the heart, thymus, and heart chakra is so vital, however, that I will discuss the thymus in the next section.

Your heart is a fist-sized muscle that pumps blood twenty-four hours a day. It is made of four parts: two atria on the top and two ventricles on the bottom. It is fed by coronary arteries that run along its surface and provide oxygen-rich blood for its own use. Valves connect these chambers. Nerve tissues run through the heart, helping manage the complex signals that keep the heart beating.

Scientists have discovered that the heart is more than a circulatory organ; it is also an endocrine gland, producing and secreting a rich array of hormones and neurotransmitters. These hormones include oxytocin, the "love bonding" hormone, which is also made in the brain. The heart produces several other hormones as well, including many peptides, which are made of amino acids, the building blocks of hormones. It seems that there is also constant crosstalk between the gonads, heart hormones, and adipose tissue (fat).[3]

In recent years an entire discipline has arisen, called cardiac endocrinology, to study the important impact of the heart's hormones on the rest of the body and its many organ systems. About a dozen heart hormone secretions govern many aspects of your health. These rather recently discovered hormones include interleukin-33, which affects your inflammatory responses, and microRNA, noncoding RNA molecules that serve as biomarkers for cardiovascular diseases.[4]

Because of its unique capabilities, the heart operates almost like a brain unto itself, transmitting signals sent to the brain along the spinal column and the vagus nerve,

3 Aldo Clerico et al., "Thirty Years of the Heart as an Endocrine Organ: Physiological Role and Clinical Utility of Cardiac Natriuretic Hormones," *Heart and Circulatory Physiology* (July 1, 2011), https://journals.physiology.org/doi/full/10.1152/ajpheart.00226.2011.

4 Juanjuan Zhao and Liming Pei, "Cardiac Endocrinology: Heart-Derived Hormones in Physiology and Disease," *Basic to Translational Science* 5, no. 9 (2020): 949–960.

the longest nerve in your body. Because of this, it's constantly influencing your nervous and endocrine systems, digestive and urinary tracts, spleen, respiratory and lymph systems, and numerous brain activities. Compared to the brain, it seems the heart is an equal force in determining your health, if not sometimes an even greater one. In fact, it emanates an electrical field that is sixty times stronger than the field the brain generates. Furthermore, the magnetic field it generates is one hundred times vaster than the field created by the brain, encoding every single atom, molecule, cell, organ, and organ system with data to formulate health—or not.[5]

As we'll explore further in chapter 3, it pays to be heart happy. Positive emotions cause the heart to produce optimum effects in your body; they also improve your financial earning power and relationships. Conversely, challenging emotions such as fear and anger negatively affect all aspects of your life. The well-substantiated research that demonstrates these effects suggests that the ancients really were right: all good things come from love.[6]

---

5   HeartMath Institute, "Science of the Heart: Exploring the Role of the Heart in Human Performance," https://www.heartmath.org/research/science-of-the-heart/.

6   HeartMath Institute, "HeartMath Institute Science: Scientific Foundation of the HeartMath System," https://www.heartmath.org/science/.

SECONDARY ENDOCRINE
GLAND: THE THYMUS

As I mentioned earlier, many systems consider the thymus as the hormone gland for anahata. This fascinating organ is located in the center of the upper chest, between the lungs and behind the sternum, above and in front of the heart. Consisting of two lobes that join in front of the trachea, it processes many of the white blood cells produced in the bone marrow and converts them into T cells.

T cells help orchestrate the immune system, scanning for abnormalities and infections and rousing the response of the entire immune system when they find them. It is interesting that the thymus gland is active during gestation through puberty, when it begins to shrink. For instance, it weighs 15 grams at birth, 35 grams during puberty, 25 grams at age twenty-five, less than 15 grams at age sixty, and about 6 grams at seventy years of age.[7] At this point, it is little more than fatty tissue. But the thymus is so important that branches of medicine are now trying to rescue it from its shrinking-violet plight to aid in everything from anti-aging to immune strengthening.

To boost the thymus, people use holistic methods such as tapping and supplementation. The medical community

7   New World Encyclopedia, "Thymus," https://www
.newworldencyclopedia.org/entry/Thymus.

is seeking solutions such as administering certain growth factors and hormones as well as gamma chains like specific forms of interleukin. Researchers are also inhibiting sex steroids to regrow the thymus gland as well as bioengineering the thymus for improved function.[8]

In some circles the thymus is called the "high heart" and considered integral to a maturing humanity. In other systems it is perceived as another major chakra and at the least a minor one. In my twelve-chakra system, the thymus is the hormone gland associated with the eighth or shamanic chakra, which occupies a space above the head and can be seen in the figure on page 22. It is also believed to be an etheric center or an emerging transpersonal chakra that enables spiritual growth.

One of my favorite energy medicine experts of all time is Richard Gerber, author of *Vibrational Medicine*. According to Dr. Gerber, the thymus gland is a minor chakra, but it is also influenced by the activity of the heart chakra. Even though the thymus decreases in size as we age, Dr. Gerber points out that it continues to produce hormones, including thymosins, that affect our immunity.

---

8   Mohammed S. Chaudry et al., "Thymus: The Next (Re)Generation," *Immunological Reviews* vol. 271,1 (2016): 56–71, https://doi.org/10.1111/imr.12418.

One of its many essential roles is to keep certain lymphocytes in check so that our protective cells will only attack dangerous invaders or cancer cells, not our own cells.[9] When these cells don't function or function insufficiently, we develop autoimmune dysfunctions. There are more than eighty known types of autoimmune dysfunctions, conditions in which our immune "drill sergeants" attack our own cells instead of foreign marauders or our own mutated cells (which can develop into cancer). Autoimmune disorders include many cancers, heart disease, chronic fatigue, and arthritis.

RELATED PHYSICAL STRESSORS, PROBLEMS, AND ILLNESSES

Physical illnesses related to anahata include diseases of the heart, lungs, breasts, pericardium, and ribs, including heart disease, asthma, cancers, and pneumonia; thoracic spinal issues; and problems with the thymus, upper back, shoulders, and arms, all the way to the fingertips.

In terms of symptoms, you might track signs of a stressed immune system, such as being constantly sick with colds and flus. Heart arrhythmias, poor circulation, blood pressure problems, and respiratory and breathing issues are also com-

9   Richard Gerber, *Vibrational Medicine* (Rochester, VT: Bear & Company, third edition, 2001), 378–82.

mon fourth chakra challenges. So are issues with the breasts, including cancers and fibrous tissue.

SARS-CoV-2, more commonly known as COVID-19, commonly impacts the lungs, but it can also lead to heart and other vascular issues. Long COVID is one name given to the ongoing impact of COVID-19 on the heart, lungs, and other bodily tissues, often only diagnosable through symptoms such as breathing and heart irregularities, exhaustion, and the formation of blood clots.

SUMMARY

Your heart chakra is the central controller of all the bodily organs and functions found in your chest. From cardiovascular to respiratory functions, it is a critical piece for creating good health, often determining the healthy functioning of your other organ systems.

Located in the cardiac plexus, this chakra mainly depends on the well-being of its major endocrine gland, the heart, as well as on the role played by its secondary endocrine gland, the thymus. Imbalances can impact any area of your life, which means it is vital to take care of your heart so it can take care of you.

Now it's time to delve into all things psychological regarding your heart chakra.

3

OF THE PSYCHE AND THE SOUL

This chapter is all about the psychology and soul of your fourth chakra, which is rich in both ideas and ideals.

The word *psychology* comprises two words: psyche (or "soul") and logos (or "study"). Here we'll explore the psychology of your fourth chakra through the various emotions and beliefs that move through it and are imprinted upon it. We'll also look at the ways in which your soul inhabits and expresses through your fourth chakra; put another way, we'll be discussing spirituality. In fact, as you'll see, your silent love chakra is all important in enabling the embodiment of your essence, or spirit.

We'll begin by delving into anahata's general psychological tasks. We'll then do a meet and greet of your heart chakra's other fascinating facets, including the age at which it activates, its associated archetypes, and the types of intuitive abilities that are available through it. I'll also more completely link the roles of the physical heart and thymus in making sure you're psychologically and spiritually fit.

OVERARCHING PSYCHOLOGICAL IMPACT

Ideally, the heart chakra is the center of all positive emotions as well as virtues such as appreciation and compassion. Considered the center of love in most religions and spiritual disciplines, it regulates our relationships with self, others, and the Divine. Within this center we learn to balance our own emotional and relationship needs with those of others, seeking to be generous but also self-caring, nurturing but also ethical, individualistic yet communal. No matter one's gender, the location of the breasts within the heart chakra area speak to our innate ability to nourish and nurture others, especially those in need.

Anahata is also associated with our ability to escape the limitations of karma and make decisions honoring the bindings of the past even as we are transcending them. To "follow our heart" is to perceive and create choices from a higher place rather than our lower chakra nature, which is based on desires and compulsions.

Within our heart we learn to balance opposites—male and female, mind and body, ego and unity. We therefore confront the qualities that oppose unconditional love, such as jealousy, envy, and hatred. Along the way we eventually learn to embrace and embody our true spiritual identity.

CHAKRA ACTIVATION

Every chakra awakens at a different time during our development from infancy to adulthood. It's as if it goes into high gear while simultaneously becoming super absorbent. This is so we can program it as fully as possible during that stage. Into it go the feelings, ideas, beliefs, and even memories of events large and small that relate to that chakra's bandwidth. This programming allows the chakra to carry on physically, psychologically, and spiritually.

As you might expect, some of the love-based data streams encoded in your heart chakra are beneficial. Others are not; there is a reason so many people repeat the same addictions or relationships they saw as children. It's extraordinarily important to sort through the ideals that are playing house in your heart chakra. You'll want to retain some, refurbish others, and discard many.

Your fourth chakra activates between the ages of four and a half and eight and a half. This is a long, milestone-rich phase. During this time the typical child jumps from preschool and being home based to the initial grades of elementary school. As these years unfold, the child shifts from being mainly involved with and loyal to family members and starts to form friendships of their own. They become increasingly independent in terms of their daily care, such as selecting desirable snacks or outfits or first sports, getting set up to take on more and more of their own decision making.

It's vital that their caretakers provide them a full sampling of life teachings and activities at this time. On the docket are establishing safe boundaries and figuring out how to choose healthy foods. If screen time is limited and the family engages in a loving way, the heart chakra can expand and find wonderful and sometimes even unusual sources of love, from a family pet to a favorite tree to a great school friend.

In general, the parameters that will impact a child's views about love become distinct during these years. If they learn to accept others regardless of race, gender, or sexual and gender identity, they will be able to meet people where they are as adults. If they become entrenched in judgments and observe cruelty, they might be reluctant to enter into relationships or cope by adopting the same negative behaviors they are witnessing.

From a chakra system perspective, the fourth chakra opens after the third chakra is turned on, following the activation of the second and first chakras' training wheels. Any earlier programming can support or stunt the developing heart chakra.

PSYCHOLOGICAL FUNCTIONS

In the last chapter, I emphasized the important role the heart organ, and therefore the heart chakra, plays in our psychological self. While physically the heart contains 40,000 neurons and possesses the ability to process, learn, and remember, it also employs its own emotions. When we're focused on emotions that engage the soul in a sustaining and positive way, such as compassion and gratitude, the brain can achieve higher cognitive functions. It can self-regulate, and we achieve what's called heart-brain coherence. Sure, we might be struck at times by triggering events and despairing or anxious feelings, but we can quickly rebalance, and our overall physical and psychological health will remain steady and beneficial.

When we spend too much time in emotions such as frustration and anxiety, however, the physical heart beats erratically. The brain descends into thoughts including shame and fear-based ideas, and we make frenzied decisions.[10] We just plain feel worse about ourselves and the world.

10 Jessica I. Morales, "The Heart's Electromagnetic Field Is Your Superpower," *Psychology Today* (November 29, 2020), https://www.psychologytoday.com/us/blog/building-the-habit-hero/202011/the-hearts-electromagnetic-field-is-your-superpower.

The thymus is also affected by the types of emotions we hold—or don't hold—in our heart chakra. According to Dr. Gerber, whom we introduced in the previous chapter, medical researchers have yet to realize that the flow of prana through the heart chakra determines the function of the thymus and therefore our body's immune competence. Just as the heart responds to emotions, the thymus reacts positively or negatively to the emotions of the heart. In a nutshell, limiting emotions in the heart can set us up for autoimmune disorders. Dr. Gerber believes the key to a healthy heart and thymus is love of self.[11]

So how can you naturally boost your thymus? Sound therapy, tapping, and chanting can help; so can using gemstones, including turquoise and aquamarine. Beneficial foods such as fruits and vegetables and exercise and sleep are imperative. Challenges to thymus health include emotional stressors, malnutrition, environmental factors, alcoholism, and long-term physical problems.

PSYCHOLOGICAL DEFICIENCIES IN AN UNHEALTHY FOURTH CHAKRA

Deficiencies in anahata include the inability to forgive, loneliness, lack of empathy, lack of self-love, apathy, indifference, and withdrawing or becoming aimless. These types

11 Gerber, *Vibrational Medicine*, 372–82.

of problems are often caused by shadow (or hidden) emotions that impact our sense of love and lovability. Especially if we have experienced a lot of rejection or abandonment in our lives—or an acute event causing either issue—we lose the hope that we will be embraced for our entire self. That last statement is the key to finding ourselves in healthy friendships and romantic relationships, which depend on good behavior, yes, but also on full acceptance. The walls created by feeling bad about ourselves will continue to rise until we don't even know how to break out of them.

Overindulging in the negative side effects of relationships can lead to its own set of concerns, such as jealousy, codependency, martyrdom, self-aggrandizement, egotism, self-centeredness, and tribalism. We might drive ourselves forward, feeling sorry for ourselves while either caretaking others excessively or doing the opposite (taking advantage of others) because we don't know how to rest in the abode of self-care and appreciation inside ourselves. No matter our challenge, it is essential to create a nest of silent self-love within our heart chakra and get in touch with the authentic self within this haven as often as possible.

PSYCHOLOGICAL STRENGTHS
IN THE HEALTHY FOURTH CHAKRA

Anahata in balance creates a sense of wholeness and a host of love-centered abilities including empathy, compassion, friendliness, motivation, nurturing, and acceptance. It especially enables our ability to live by—and through—two essential spiritual qualities: compassion and forgiveness.

The heart chakra is capable of great suffering and pain but also enormous love and understanding. When we're compassionate toward self and others, the heart stretches. Sure, it might sometimes feel like it's going to break or maybe burst into pieces and scatter. But it doesn't, and won't if we remember that everyone is doing their best to figure out how to love. And if it's just too hard to hold it all in, don't. Share what is causing conflict and decide to heal your own wounds. We can only change ourselves.

Forgiveness is the capacity to move on. It involves surrendering, letting go, and accepting what has been, whether we are injured irrevocably or able to transform. Ultimately, it involves releasing the energetic charges of a situation so we can return to a balanced state.

Forgiveness does not require forgetting. If we have harmed ourselves or another, we want to remember what caused the damage and do our best to not repeat that action or maintain that attitude. If another grieves us, we want to establish necessary boundaries but also stay open to attracting the right types of love.

Sometimes it is impossible to forgive. That's okay. Following is a short practice that will enable a release anyway.

FORGIVING WHEN YOU CAN'T

Perhaps you are simply too badly hurt. Maybe you've wounded yourself too often to be okay with yourself. Maybe another person or situation has caused you so much harm that you don't want to forgive, so don't. Do this instead.

Focus on the circumstances that are so horrifying that every cell in your body refuses to move on. Then think of whatever you call your Higher Power. Ask that this being simply take the situation from you—lock, stock, and barrel—and perform forgiveness for you. Trust that this will occur in perfect timing. If you ever want to take up the torch again to beat up yourself or another, remind yourself that you have turned the task of forgiveness over to a higher consciousness.

ASSOCIATED ARCHETYPES

An archetype is a template or model. There are positive and negative archetypes associated with the fourth chakra.

The fourth chakra is enforced by the lover archetype. This brand of being seeks emotion and connection and is often led by passions including joy, sexual charge, and enthusiasm. Ultimately, the most amazing lover seeks pleasure for self as well as for others.

The detracting archetype is that of actor. All too often the actor is self-seeking, using their ability to read others' desires and emotions to change their own moods and personality. Unless they are careful, they will lose touch with their own heart and soul and become a chameleon.

The following short exercise will help you sense the difference between operating as a lover and as an actor.

PRACTICE

TRY ON YOUR FOURTH CHAKRA ARCHETYPES

Think of a relationship you'd like to improve. It doesn't need to be romantic, although it might be. A friendship, work partner, or relative—anyone of value to your heart is in relationship with you.

In a reflective space, imagine yourself as this person's lover. You are embodying all aspects of being a higher embodiment of your soul and are able to provide and receive unconditional love. You are also meticulous about operating within the bounds of the relationship. If this is a sexual relationship, you can easily move to intimate passion. If you're thinking of a deep soul mate, you can exchange emotions and ideas in a safe way.

Now imagine that you're playing the part of an actor in this relationship. You dress the part of the people pleaser because, essentially, you want to get your way. How do you picture your actions? How do your emotions shift depending on whether or not your manipulations are successful?

Activate the clear element of air that lies within your heart and let it blow away any artifice. Decide to come from the place of your genuine self and see what occurs in that relationship.

PERSONALITY PROFILE

If you are strong in your heart chakra, you are a relater. Is there a relationship in the house? The heart-based person gravitates to couples and can tell within minutes what's working and what's not between them. If you are fourth chakra centered, love and happiness are your core values, as is the tendency to want to fix other people's relationship problems. This focus has the potential to thrust you into the world of healing and acts of serving others. Your spiritual purpose will often involve helping others relationally or through healing endeavors.

THE INTUITIVE GIFTS
OF THE FOURTH CHAKRA

In the contemporary world, the heart's major intuitive gift is called relational empathy. Put in simple terms, you know what is occurring in others' relationships and what deeper desires they hold for love. This puts you in the strong position of being able to counsel others—and yourself—about the need for love.

This can be a challenging gift because you might easily slip into codependency. That is the tendency to do for others what they should actively be doing for themselves. That practice will leave you exhausted, dismayed, and often angry. In a codependent relationship where you're giving and not being given to, you'll eventually become resentful.

The solution is to activate another deeper gift inherent in the heart chakra: healing. To heal is to invite the change that will encourage more love. You don't need to be a doctor or a therapist to be all about love, though you certainly might be. By holding graciousness and compassion toward self and other, you serve as a healer, and the world certainly needs more of that. A healer doesn't push another's boundaries. They leave them in their situation unless it is comfortable to assist. A healer is devoted to the long haul of love.

A FEW OTHER EXTRAORDINARY
SPIRITUAL ABILITIES

The ancient Hindus had an entire list of wild, out-there abilities associated with the heart chakra. These are especially associated with the activation of the rising kundalini through the fourth chakra.

In Hinduism these are known as *siddhis*. The word embraces a wide variety of rather miraculous capabilities that occur with the higher awareness of love. The *anahata siddhi,* or extraordinary powers, activate upon achieving full control of the element of air. They include the *bhuchari siddhi* (ability to travel anywhere), *khechari siddhi* (flight through the sky), and the *kaya siddhi* (transcending old age, disease, and death).

And there are even more aptitudes to add to this list. Consider immeasurable knowledge; knowledge of the past, present, and future; and clairaudience and clairvoyance. Besides this, the anahata yogi can discover cures for various illnesses, understand physiological matters, create and destroy the obvious, and make gold and find hidden treasures. In addition, the flowering of the heart activates other higher gifts, including the ability to hear speech from a distance; assume other forms; enter another's body, whether they are alive or dead; die at will; participate in the sports of the gods in heaven; and experience no obstruction to their command.

I invite you to investigate which of these heart abilities might open for you.

SUMMARY

Anahata is full of splendid soul wonders, psychological abilities that create clear and streamlined relationships. Given your ability to continue advancing into self- and other love, it imparts self-care along with an aptitude for compassion and forgiveness. When lacking these traits, it's all too easy to fall into isolationism, codependency, or greed. Because one of anahata's innate intuitive abilities is healing, however, you can restore yourself to good grace and renew your heart again. Lean into the lover rather than the actor archetype to enjoy everything the silent love chakra has to offer.

PART 2

APPLYING FOURTH CHAKRA
KNOWLEDGE IN REAL LIFE

• • • • • •

Now it's time to synchronize your heartbeat to joy. Here in part 2, the second stage of your grand fourth chakra adventure, you will learn numerous ways to benefit from the rich resources that are available to you through your silent love chakra and begin to actively use this knowledge to realize your dreams.

Every single one of the upcoming chapters has been brilliantly formulated by an author who has deep knowledge of anahata's energy. All have explored their own anahata chakras individually but have also helped others with their fourth chakra concerns as professionals in their fields. If I might speak for them, their highest desire is to enable you to fully embrace the power of your fourth chakra.

You can enjoy these chapters in any order, beginning wherever your interest takes you. Perhaps you want to immediately learn what to cook to boost your fourth chakra. Waiting for you near the end of part 2 is a chapter featuring two chefs; go ahead and indulge in their delicious recipes. Maybe you'd rather start by meeting a few spirit allies or figure out which vibrational remedies or crystals to select to spark specific transformations. Whatever you need to rock and roll into the very heart of your inner heart, it's all right here.

YOU'LL BE USING INTENTION

Many of the ideas and practices presented in part 2 will make use of a relatively commonplace but extraordinarily effective process: establishing an intention. For this reason, I want to introduce you to this concept and provide a few tips for how to create an intention.

An intention is like a desire with a punch. Think about how many times you dream and dream again about the same desired future scenario. Eventually, you must decide whether you want that wish to come true or whether you will simply return it to the land of maybe. When you formulate a longing and then go for it, it's as if it grows legs and comes alive.

When you use intention, you are inviting subtle energies to the party. We have already established that almost 100 percent of all energy is subtle. Initializing your chakras, auric fields, and entire subtle self with a focused desire adds magic to the mix.

In a way, everything that exists in the world is a manifestation of intention. This takes many forms: prayers, hopes, daydreams, and even ambitions. The truth is that everything concrete had its origins in a creative impulse or an empowered intention. This means that at one level, intention is nothing more or less than packaging an inspiration in a way that enables it to come true.

The easiest way to fashion an intention is to formulate a statement of desire. This activity occurs in three steps.

Begin by composing a one-sentence statement that summarizes what you want. It's back to English class for you, as this sentence requires the combination of at least one noun (subject) and a verb (action). Then you must tack on the actual desire. Set this wish in present-day time and use words that are optimistic and life enhancing. For instance, imagine that you long to go deep sea diving. You could create an intention like this one:

I am loving my hobby as a deep sea diver.

Second, you must sprinkle emotion into your intention. Think like this.

My intention has already occurred.

I am living the dream.

*Wow, everything packed into that
tiny sentence is happening.*

Directing your emotion into your intention puts the energies in motion toward your goal.

The third step involves repeating your intention until it turns into a decision, not only a part of your heart's wish list. Focus on it daily. Put it to song and dance. Turn it into a poem or recite it every time you enter your bedroom.

Above all, be happy that this dream has sprung into your physical reality.

I'd love to have you practice creating an intention this very minute—after all, practice makes perfect. You can keep practicing with any of the chapters in part 2.

Focus on a desire aligned with your silent love chakra. Maybe you're interested in matters of love, physiological healing, clearing up a relationship issue, or simply becoming more heart based. Next, frame your aspiration into a statement you would like to vitalize. Try something like this:

I am in love with life itself and
continually guided by the Spirit.

You can employ this inspirational statement like a mantra or a poem; sing it in the shower or share it with your friends. If it feels like this goal might require a bit more pizzazz, simply formulate a related intention and put it to play—and to work.

And remember, the heart is ultimately about joy. Make it a point to notice the changes in your life and even greater happiness will come your way.

4

SPIRIT ALLIES

MARGARET ANN LEMBO

Love, kindness, and compassion are the focus! The heart chakra is relationship centered, which means that it responds to loving connections, not only with people and animals, but also with the amazing types of invisible beings that are available to a benevolent heart. The wide array of spirit allies means the list of benefits is broad: receiving assistance to enable healing, enjoying spiritual experiences, promoting more goodness on earth, and more.

There are many spirit allies that can help you enliven your heart chakra, igniting your inner self so that you can better extend into the world. The information in this chapter will bring you into the center of your heart by tapping into the support of metaphysical assistants.

Let's get familiar with the energies of these invisible helpers so you can be discerning and invite only those that are working for your highest good. Spirit allies exist in many forms: angels and archangels, plant spirits or the devic forces of essential oils, and animal and gemstone guardians. (Also refer to my section about working with crystals and gemstones in chapter 10.)

ANGELS, ANIMAL ALLIES, AND DEVIC FORCES

When I was a child, I realized that plants have consciousness, thanks to the time I spent talking and listening to the plants and flowers in my mother's garden. Energy and vibration are in every plant and flower as well as other aspects of nature.

The seen and unseen are equally real. Spirit allies genuinely help guide and light our path. When we let in their influence, we can receive love from all of nature. To gain insights and healings from natural beings, we use telepathy, or intuitive connection. Luckily, our imagination, prompted by visualization or empathy or both, can enable our telepathic abilities. Heart-centered communication from nature then flows through us as we ourselves are part of nature and are always bonded with it.

When applying this intuitive ability to the fourth chakra in particular, remember that it is a bridge within you that connects you to heaven and earth. Love, kindness, tolerance, and compassion are the focus of the heart chakra. You can work with the spirit allies I will describe next to enable the exchange of love, which is actually your true nature.

ANGELS AND ARCHANGELS

Your angelic helpers act and react based on your thoughts, prayers, and petitions for assistance. They are messengers of the Divine. Permit them to inspire you with guidance and wisdom. These beings of light, color, and vibration are androgynous. I'll introduce you to several angels and one archangel. Archangels are more powerful and have greater reach compared to other types of angels.

Angel of Compassion

Compassion and empathy are essential components of the heart chakra. Ask the Angel of Compassion to open your heart and your consciousness so you can bring comfort and mercy to the people in your life. Call on the Angel of Compassion to help you notice when you need to show greater compassion for yourself, and when you do need it, set a kindhearted intention to do so.

Remember that your true nature is love, and you can choose how you respond to other people. Instead of reacting to unpleasant people, take a moment to breathe and say a little prayer for them and yourself. As you send off a request for assistance from this angel, clearly envision that confidence.

AFFIRMATIONS: I am empathic. I am compassionate and kind. I am blessed to have thoughtful, loving people around me. I am mindful to communicate in a way where my words are caring. I live with love, I act with compassion, and I practice acceptance in all that I do.

Angel of Unconditional Love

With this angel on your team, you can recognize that many people love you exactly as you are, without judgment. The Angel of Unconditional Love is an ally for you when you need to apologize or forgive (or both). Let this angel help you hone your ability to release resentment, anger, or negativity toward yourself or another person. This angel can help guide you to demonstrate your love to others and yourself. Permit the Angel of Unconditional Love to activate loving-kindness. Send a petition requesting assistance to this angel to help you recognize love in its many forms.

AFFIRMATIONS: My consciousness is aligned with loving-kindness. Inner peace is healing. I radiate love through my eyes. I offer forgiveness through words and actions.

Guardian Angel

Call on your guardian angel when you need help in any situation. Your guardian angel has been by your side since birth and will remain with you throughout life. This angel's mission is to protect and guide you. Remember to ask for help and be specific about what you need. All you must do is think these thoughts with your guardian angel in mind, and help will be on the way.

Connect with the loving support of your guardian angel and know that you are never alone. Open your mind to notice the symbols this celestial being sends your way, and interpret its messages to make your everyday life easier. Comfort, kindness, and love are the reasons your guardian angel is always by your side. To emphasize your request for help, you can repeat this traditional petition:

> *Angel of God, my guardian dear,*
> *to whom God's love commits you here.*
> *Ever this day be at my side*
> *to light and guard, to rule and guide.*

AFFIRMATIONS: An angel shines a light on my path. I am grateful for the inspiration from the Divine. It is easy for me to deal with any situation. I am blessed with supportive people, places, and situations.

Archangel Jophiel

Call on Archangel Jophiel to help you remember to take the time to observe the beauty and blessings in your surroundings. Gratitude is key to an open heart chakra. Let Jophiel help you become a conduit for allowing heaven and earth to meet at your center. Acknowledge the essence of the divine love within you. Connect with Archangel Jophiel in a fragrant garden or through a bouquet of cut flowers. This archangel can help you remember to stop and smell the roses and delight in the joys of nature.

Call on Jophiel to help you increase your ability to be courteous and kind. The heart chakra is where you hold the energy of divine love, friendship, romance, and love in every definition of the word. It is the place where you deal with how you are in a relationship. It is a good place to focus when connecting with beauty and gratitude while maintaining heart-centered awareness.

> **AFFIRMATIONS:** I am filled with love. I realize that love surrounds me at all times. Only goodness and blessings are allowed in my space. Wherever I am, love is. I am happy! I have nurturing experiences everywhere I go.

ANIMAL ALLIES

The connectedness of everything on our planet—from rocks and crystals to plants and animals—links messages and lessons from the animal kingdom with your consciousness to benefit your personal awareness and growth. Here are a few animal allies that can bring you messages and realizations on your spiritual journey.

Duck

The mandarin duck is the ultimate symbol of love and marriage in Southeast Asia. It is said that these ducks are faithful, lifelong mates and good luck symbols for a happy marriage. The image or figurine of a mandarin duck is used in classical feng shui to adjust the energetic environment to improve love relationships. Duck medicine is helpful when you want to relax into your feelings and emotions and enjoy being with your family.

> **AFFIRMATIONS:** I am gentle with myself. I realize that kindheartedness brings about better circumstances. Kindness and compassion are a normal way of being for me. I attract healthy, harmonious relationships.

Flamingo

When flamingo wades into your life, perhaps it is time to consider spending a day at the shore's edge, walking in the water with friends or a beloved sweetheart. This ally is especially useful when you are ready to enjoy a heart-centered activity in the company of good friends and large groups of like-minded people. Flamingo is also the perfect ally to call on to attract a monogamous life partner.

> **AFFIRMATIONS:** I act from my heart chakra. Loving experiences are naturally drawn into my life. I am grateful for the blessing of romantic love.

Swan

Swan is an ally that helps you live harmoniously and at home in your spiritual consciousness while walking on this earthly physical plane. When swan glides into your life, let it help you attract a healthy romantic relationship; supportive, loving friendships; and ethical business colleagues. Develop and cultivate a personal practice of kindness, compassion, and tolerance for yourself and all beings.

> **AFFIRMATIONS:** I am graceful while I stand in my personal power. I am balanced. My body is tranquil and peaceful. I am elegant and flow with life.

AROMATHERAPEUTIC ALLIES

Aromatherapy is the use of essential oils derived from the aromatic parts of plants. It is usually delivered in the form of oils, mists, incense, or sprays to heal physical, mental, and emotional complaints and improve overall well-being. It is important to establish an intention and access the unlimited potential of your imagination when working with aromatherapy to balance your chakras. Here are a few beneficial essential oils for awakening the heart chakra energy center.

Grapefruit

Grapefruit essential oil, especially the pink variety, helps open your heart to receive blessings, joy, and happiness. It evokes bliss and comfort. Use this oil to rid your emotional body of doubt and fear. Trust that you can develop loving relationships with this oil in your energy field. Use grapefruit to return to joy after periods of grief.

> **AFFIRMATIONS:** I radiate light and good energy. I move forward with the courage to live to my full potential. My heart is open to love.

> **FOR YOUR SAFETY:** This oil is phototoxic; therefore, avoid exposure to direct sunlight when using it topically.

Rose

Rose is a reminder that love is the answer to everything. Use rose to radiate love in a wide circumference around your being. Since the heart chakra is the center of your consciousness, love is who you truly are. Rose is helpful in your meditation practice for expanding your sphere of love.

> **AFFIRMATIONS:** I attract love, joy, and happiness. I feel reassured. Blessings are showing up in my world. I am blessed.

> **FOR YOUR SAFETY:** There are no known contraindications except that it is best not to use rose oil during the first trimester of pregnancy.

Sweet Marjoram

Sweet marjoram helps you release subconscious fears and remind you of your faith. Attract happiness and harmony while inhaling its aroma. You'll start to see an increase in the number of loyal and caring friends in your life as soon as you decide to accept that love. Allow the development of a new romantic relationship or the rekindling of an existing one. According to Greek mythology, Aphrodite is credited with bringing sweet marjoram into creation, and its use in Egypt dates to 1000 BCE. Both the Greeks and Romans crowned couples with sweet marjoram at their weddings.

AFFIRMATIONS: I see life clearly. Past experiences bring wisdom and knowledge that positively affect the here and now. I have an open heart. My emotions are balanced.

FOR YOUR SAFETY: Avoid in cases of low blood pressure. Do not use if you are pregnant or nursing.

SUMMARY

You will improve your awareness of your heart chakra by working with your spirit allies; the major message they deliver is that you are never alone. Feel and enjoy the vibration of the energies in all life. Align with the vibrations that match your mood and the moment, and let them help you. You'll enjoy the process and find that your life becomes more meaningful and interesting.

5

YOGA POSES

AMANDA HUGGINS

In yoga, each chakra is associated with specific poses that help balance and activate its energy. For example, grounding postures are used to activate the first chakra; hip openers unleash the emotions stored in the second; and twists draw out empowered energy in the third. Naturally, then, the postures meant to activate the fourth chakra are heart openers.

Heart-opening poses encompass a range of postures specifically designed to unveil, broaden, and expand the center of the heart space. These poses work to create a deep opening in the chest area, in turn inviting a profound sense of vulnerability and connection. When we engage in heart-opening yoga poses, we cultivate an opportunity to connect with our emotional core, allowing us to experience greater ease in both body and mind.

In this chapter I'm going to discuss various fourth chakra yoga poses that will perfectly activate and enhance that amazing silent love chakra in the center of your chest.

KEY CONCEPTS AND TIPS FOR AWAKENING YOUR HEART CHAKRA THROUGH YOGA

On a physical level, opening the heart chakra means engaging and stretching the muscles in the chest, shoulders, and upper back. Heart-opening poses target these areas to release tension and tightness, creating space and freedom for the heart center. As these poses open the chest, they also encourage deep and expansive breathing, enhancing the flow throughout the body of oxygen and prana (the Sanskrit term for life force energy). Heart openers also promote healthy circulation and blood flow, which can be particularly beneficial for the cardiovascular system. By stimulating the heart, these poses may also help regulate blood pressure and improve overall heart health.

In the modern world, the demands of daily life often cause us to inadvertently close off our heart chakra. The prevalence of prolonged sitting or hunching over computers and phone screens combined with the subconscious act of turning inward toward our screens can manifest physically as discomfort and stiffness in the upper body. Heart-stretching yoga poses offer a counteraction to this turned-in lifestyle, inviting us to consciously reverse these patterns. By lengthening the spine and broadening the chest, we create a physical release that translates into an energetic shift. As the chest expands and the heart space opens, we provide much-needed relief of tension in the upper body. Releasing tension in the chest and shoulders supports our spinal health and allows us to breathe more freely and deeply. The space that's created when we're able to physically expand our heart space supports the reawakening of the heart chakra, allowing its energy to flow freely once again. Through the practice of heart-engaging poses, we harmonize the physical and energetic realms, restoring balance to the body and facilitating a deeper connection to our own heart-centered essence.

Practicing self-compassion is an integral aspect of heart-centered yoga. Many of us struggle with self-criticism and a lack of self-love, and it's not uncommon for those traits to show up on our yoga mats. As you flow through the poses and navigate the physical and emotional sensations that arise, you may encounter moments of self-criticism or judgment. It's important to recognize that these inner dialogues are remnants of old patterns that no longer serve you.

The lessons that show up on your mat are metaphors for the rest of your life. Yoga encourages you to be gentle with yourself, accept your imperfections, and recognize your inherent worthiness. When you notice self-criticism arising during your practice, view it as an invitation for self-compassion. Instead of getting caught up in the negativity, gently redirect your attention to your heart space. With each breath and movement, remind yourself that your practice is a safe and sacred space for growth and self-discovery. Treat yourself with the same kindness and understanding that you would offer to a dear friend.

Self-compassion is not about perfection or eradicating all negative thoughts. It's about creating a nurturing inner environment where you can flourish. By embracing self-compassion on your mat, you are cultivating a foundation of self-love that extends beyond your practice and into every aspect of your life. Each pose becomes an opportunity to practice patience, forgiveness, and acceptance, all qualities that support your journey toward a more loving relationship with yourself. As you continue to weave self-compassion into your heart-centered yoga practice, you'll find that the seeds of self-love you sow on the mat blossom into a radiant and enduring sense of well-being. The practice of self-compassion is an act of self-care, a gentle reminder that you are worthy of your own kindness. Through the union of heart-centered yoga and self-compassion, you are nurturing a profound connection with your heart chakra.

PRACTICE

FOURTH CHAKRA YOGA FLOW

This practice can be conducted in a flow, meaning one pose follows another without necessarily holding each pose. You can also hold yourself in any one of the poses at a separate time, depending on your needs. For instance, if you only have a few moments in the morning to ground yourself, you can simply hold the first one in this series, child's pose, during that time.

As you prepare for your practice, consider the intentions suggested below as gentle guidance to spark your own heartfelt aspirations. Feel free to select the ones that deeply resonate with you, allowing them to shape your practice into a profound journey of self-discovery and love. With each inhalation and exhalation, let your intentions infuse your movements and breath, cultivating a nurturing and transformative experience that radiates from your heart space.

> » I intend to open my heart fully, allowing love and compassion to flow effortlessly within and around me.

> » I set the intention to release any grudges or resentments, allowing forgiveness to heal and free my heart.

» I embrace vulnerability as a source of strength and authenticity, opening myself to deeper connections and experiences.

» My intention is to shower myself with unconditional love and acceptance, recognizing my worthiness and value.

» I intend to release any past hurts or emotional baggage, making space for healing and emotional renewal.

» I aim to radiate compassion not only toward others but also toward myself, nurturing a kind, gentle inner dialogue.

As you move through the following flow, focus on cultivating feelings of love, compassion, and self-acceptance. Imagine your heart center expanding with each breath, radiating love outward to yourself and those around you.

You'll want to engage the following poses on a yoga mat or another cushioned, flat surface such as a soft carpet.

» begin in child's pose

Start in a kneeling position, sitting back on your heels. Stretch your arms forward and lower your chest toward the mat, resting your forehead on the ground. Take several deep breaths here, allowing your heart to relax. With each breath in, imagine filling up your heart space with bright, loving, vibrant energy. With each breath out, imagine that energy cleansing away any blockages in the heart space.

» flow into tabletop position

On an inhale, come onto your hands and knees in a tabletop position. To accomplish this, place your hands underneath your shoulders and spread your fingers wide. Keep your hands parallel to each other. Bring your knees under your hips, keeping them hip-width distance, and place the tops of your feet flat on your mat. Tuck your chin toward your chest. You are now in a pose resembling a tabletop.

» shift into cow and cat pose

Exhale and hold that tabletop pose. On your next inhale, let your belly sink down, lift your tailbone, and gaze upward for cow pose. Feel the broadening of the heart space as you shine the center of your chest open.

Exhale, round your spine up, tuck your chin to your chest, and curl your tailbone under for cat pose. Repeat this flow with your breath for a few rounds, experimenting with the sensations of opening and closing the heart space.

» move into downward-facing dog

Come back to tabletop position and then lift your hips up and back, rolling over or picking up and putting down the feet. Come into an inverted V shape with your body.

Press your palms and feet firmly into the mat, and allow your heart to melt toward your thighs. Aim to broaden and open the chest space here, and take full, deep breaths into the heart. You may also choose to let out an audible exhalation or a sigh to release any pent-up emotions in the heart.

> » move forward into plank pose

On an inhale, come out of the V shape of downward-facing dog and forward into a plank pose. Align your shoulders directly over your wrists, and engage your lower belly muscles to maintain a stable, straight line from your head to your heels. Ensure that your hips are neither lifted too high nor sagging down.

Modifications

DOWNWARD DOG: If your hamstrings are tight or your lower back feels strained, bend your knees. This will alleviate tension in the hamstrings and make it easier to maintain a long spine.

PLANK: Bring both knees to the ground to reduce the load on the upper body. Alternatively, you may keep the knees raised and come down onto the forearms instead of the palms.

» go into cobra pose

Lower yourself down onto your belly. Place your hands under your shoulders, elbows close to your body. As you inhale, press your hands lightly into the mat and lift your chest off the ground. Keep your hips grounded and shoulders relaxed. Press the top of your legs and feet into the floor to activate your core. Allow your upper back to do more of the work here than your hands—you may even test this by lifting both hands off the mat and allowing your chest to hover a few inches off the ground. Exhale to release the shape and bring your chest and head down toward the mat. Repeat cobra pose two to four more times.

» return to downward-facing dog

Flow back into tabletop position and then lift your hips up and back, again coming into an inverted V shape with your body. Press your palms and feet firmly into the mat and allow your heart to melt toward your thighs. Open your chest space and take full, deep breaths into the heart. You may also choose to let out an audible exhalation or sigh.

» shift back into child's pose

Return to and then stay in child's pose for three cycles of breath. Pay attention to your heartbeat, and use your exhales to bring the heart back into rest.

» find downward-facing dog again and
drop into plank position

Return to downward-facing dog, transition into plank position on an inhale, and lower yourself all the way down to the mat on an exhale.

» go into upward-facing dog

Place both palms under your shoulders, elbows close to your body. Press the palms firmly into the mat as you broaden your chest, straighten your arms, and lift your thighs and knees off the ground, pressing the tops of your feet into the mat. Lift your chest and heart toward the ceiling, keeping your legs engaged. Breathe deeply into the center of your chest for three cycles of breath. When you're finished, release the pose and lie flat on your mat for three cycles of breath.

» move into cow and cat pose again

Rise to tabletop position again and practice three to five rounds of cow and cat pose.

Modification

Instead of lifting your entire body off the ground in upward-facing dog pose, practice cobra pose again. Keep your pelvis and legs grounded while using your hands to gently lift your upper body.

» flow into camel pose

Come to a kneeling position with your toes tucked under. Place your hands on your lower back, fingers pointing downward. As you inhale, lift your chest and gently arch your back, leaning back and bringing your hands to your heels. Keep your hips aligned over your knees.

Visualize an unseen thread of energy extending from the center of your heart and ascending toward the ceiling, as if gently pulling your heart space upward. This imagery helps enhance the opening of your heart chakra during the pose.

Hold this pose for about twenty to thirty seconds. When you feel complete, release the pose and sit back on your heels. Place one hand on your heart, close your eyes, and breathe deeply as you regain your grounding.

Modification

For a gentler version of camel pose, do not release the hands to your heels. Keep your hands on your lower back for support as you gently arch your back, lifting your chest while keeping your hips aligned over your knees.

To come out of the pose, press into your forearms to lift your head and then release your back and chest down to the mat.

» go into savasana

Lie down on your back, allowing your arms and legs to relax naturally. Bring one or both hands to your heart. Close your eyes and take several deep, grounding breaths. As you exhale, visualize any remaining tension or stress leaving your body. Rest in this position for a few minutes, absorbing the benefits of your heart-opening practice.

Conclude your practice with gratitude for the time you've dedicated to opening and nurturing your heart space.

SUMMARY

The journey into heart-opening poses within your yoga practice is far more than just a physical endeavor—it is a soulful exploration that transcends the boundaries of the mat. By intentionally engaging in these postures, you invite the energies of love, compassion, and vulnerability to infuse your being, cultivating a profound connection with your heart chakra. Through this connection, you can experience enhanced self-love, emotional release, and a newfound sense of openness to the world around you.

6

BODY WISDOM

LINDSAY FAUNTLEROY

Your body is part of nature. When you attune to the natural world through your heart chakra, you will naturally achieve the highest possible levels of physical, emotional, and spiritual health. Your heart allows you to perceive the world beyond the limitations of rational and logical thinking. In this chapter I introduce practices to help you set aside rational and logical thinking for a time so that you can embody nature's wisdom.

I'd like to start by introducing you to the concept of the anima mundi. The term comes from Latin words for soul (anima) and world (mundi), or "soul of the world," and it is the shared breath and life force of all beings in the universe. Our ancestors understood that the human soul is intrinsically interconnected with the world soul. In fact, in many indigenous cultures, the heart, not the head, is the source of intelligence. Indigenous cultures and healing systems have always valued the natural world as a source of wisdom and intelligence, and here you'll be invited to do the same.

The primary way of connecting to the anima mundi is not through our logical, rational minds. We cannot listen to nature with our ears, but we can through the states of consciousness that are housed in our fourth chakra. Nature communicates through the heart by sending messages: emotions, sensations in our energetic body, and symbolic images that pop up into awareness. These imaginative, creative, and receptive states of consciousness allow us to perceive ourselves as part of an animated universe—one where birds talk, trees beckon, the river whispers, and the wind greets us with a fierce yet tender kiss. As you communicate with nature in this way, you might notice your breath lengthening, your shoulders softening, a memory resurfacing, or a sudden insight or affirmation.

ATTUNING TO NATURE'S PERCEPTION

Our modern society asks us to pay a lot of attention to our physical bodies. But as nature perceives us, it cares little about our skin color, height, or weight. In the heart of the world soul, we are essentially vibration: light and rhythm,

symbol and sound. The following exercise invites you to in-
tuit how nature experiences your presence, using its silent
love chakra as the center of awareness and perception.

> » Visit your favorite natural environment. If that
>   is not possible, open a window or commune
>   with a houseplant. Gently greet the world soul
>   with a heart-to-heart silent hello.
>
> » Breathe into your fourth chakra to imagine
>   nature as it perceives the quality of your unique
>   light. Are you a steady, warm glow; a flickering
>   flame; an excitable firework; a quiet spark? Or
>   are you a wildfire that consumes a lot of space?
>   Close your eyes and imagine nature regarding
>   you as light. Draw or sketch what you see when
>   you perceive yourself as light.
>
> » Breathe into your heart center to listen for
>   how nature might hear your presence as sound
>   reverberating through its silence. Are you an
>   up-tempo beat with an energizing pulse? Are
>   you a grounding and stabilizing heartbeat? Are
>   you rhythmic or erratic? Take a moment to
>   inwardly listen to your unique rhythm or drum
>   this rhythm on your lap, a table, or the ground.

I invite you to engage in this meditative practice anytime
you are in nature. Through your silent love chakra, notice

nature noticing you with as much attention, perception, and curiosity as those who love you most.

ACUPRESSURE: ENERGETIC POWER PORTALS

The twelve common meridians in Chinese medicine can be thought of as branches of one long river that circulates light, energy, prana, life force, consciousness, intelligence, and chi throughout the subtle body. In the West these meridians are named for the parts of our body that they intersect, and the energetic quality of each meridian changes in these landscapes. The rivers or meridians that flow from the oceanic anahata chakra are the heart, the small intestine, the triple heater, the pericardium, the lung, and the large intestine. Working with these meridians can support the fourth chakra as it opens to an infinite capacity for love and the heart-centered perception we need to see the world through ancient eyes.

PRACTICE

ACUPRESSURE FOR DYNAMIC ENERGY PORTALS

You can use all of the following acupressure points to activate the fourth chakra. You'll begin working with each in the same way.

Rest your fingertips lightly on each dynamic energy portal. Check for a subtle sense of warmth or radiance. Use a light touch; your skin should not indent under your fingertips. You can also use vibrational remedies such as tuning forks, essential oils, flower essences, and gemstones on these points. (See chapters 9 and 10 for vibrational remedies and gemstones that resonate with the fourth chakra.)

Lung 2: Yun Men (Cloud Gate)

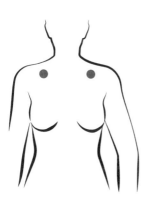

LOCATION: *Front of chest, in the triangular hollow between the pectoral muscles and deltoids.*

HOW TO FIND THIS POINT: *With fingers alongside your shoulder on the front of your chest, raise your arm slowly in front of you until you feel a triangular hollow formed by the outer edge of your clavicle, shoulder, and ribcage.*

Yun Men helps us strike a balance between two wise sayings: "In every life a little rain must fall" and "This too shall pass." True to its name, this point supports us when we experience sadness that clouds our emotional skies. As you cross your palms at the center of your chest, use the tips of your fingers to gently massage or bring attention to this point and allow the clouds to gently part as the sun re-emerges from obscurity.

Heart 1: Jiquan (Summit Spring)

LOCATION: *In the center of the armpit.*

HOW TO FIND THIS POINT: *Raise your arm above your head. Find the deepest depression at the center of the armpit. As you lower your arm, your fingers will land in this point at the height of the armpit's cave.*

After encircling the heart chakra, Jiquan is the first point on the heart meridian that is accessible at the surface of the skin. Massaging this area can help settle anxiety, sadness, and a sense of disconnection as it reconnects you to the deep wellspring of universal, cosmic, and divine love. Wrap your arms across your chest, as though giving yourself a warm hug, while tucking your hands under opposite arm-pits. Take three to five deep breaths as your emotions settle.

Pericardium 8: Laogong
(Palace of Weariness and Treasures)

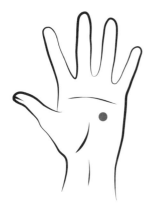

LOCATION: *Center of the palm, beneath the tip of the middle finger when making a light fist.*

HOW TO FIND THIS POINT: *Make a light fist. This point is located on the center of the palm between the index and middle fingers.*

Laogong evokes the image of a sacred temple that one can turn to for spiritual support and renewal after struggle, overwork, weariness, and suffering. This point restores your ancestral connection and your awareness of your spiritual guides' unseen support. This allows you to feel nourished and cared for despite the stress and hardships that threaten to separate you from love.

Turn your palms up toward the sky and bring your attention to the Palace of Weariness and Treasures in the center of your palms. Imagine that a small, tender flame is emerging from each palm, held in reverence as if the flames were candles on a sacred altar. Hold this reverence in your heart as you bring your palms to touch in prayer position at your heart's center. Bow deeply to the sacred force of life flowing through the world soul.

UTTARABODHI MUDRA

The uttarabodhi mudra eases an overwhelmed nervous system and brings awareness to any fear that might be blocking the heart. In addition, it is used to cultivate inspiration, focus, problem solving, and decision making by bringing clarity to the heart's knowing.

Begin by clasping the hands together, then releasing the thumb and index fingers to create a diamond shape. Bring the tips of the thumbs to the tip of your breastbone /

THE UTTAROBODHI MUDRA

sternum, where you will find a tender acupressure point called Jiewei, or Dove's Tail. This point is an ally for the uttarabodhi mudra, as it also releases grief, fear, anxiety, and emotions that cloud the clarity of the anahata chakra. Take several deep breaths, noticing as your chest expands to make space for divine love.

PRACTICE

HEART BLOSSOMING

The rose is a quintessential flower that symbolically mirrors love in all its forms. Songs like Aretha Franklin's "A Rose Is Still a Rose" and pop songstress Selena's "Como la Flor" give insight into the tender, vulnerable, and perennial nature of the love that flowers within. I am sure you can think of many other songs. This practice involves listening through your fourth/silent love chakra by paying attention to the images that emerge as you contemplate your relationships.

Begin by listing the relationships that are important to you, which might include lovers, life partners, children, family, coworkers, friends, nature, spirit, and even your relationship with yourself.

Take several deep breaths to settle into meditative contemplation as you call each relationship forward, placing your hands above your heart. Wait patiently for a floral image symbolizing this relationship to emerge in your imaginal sight. Here are a few suggested interpretations; be sure to check in with your gut-knowing for an internal sense of resonance.

Rosebud

If the flower that appears in your inner imagery is a rosebud, this may indicate a relationship that is in its early stages, where it is still too soon to know what kind of blossoming is in store. It may also indicate the need for safety, security, or protection in order to blossom, as a rosebud protects its precious vulnerability.

Blossoming Rose

A blossoming relationship is a rose in full bloom, radiating sweetness and joy. The color of the rose that appears in your heart's eye may offer insight into the type of love that dominates—or is needed—in the relationship. Red roses often suggest passion or romance; yellow roses suggest friendship and amicable camaraderie; white roses suggest connection to spirit or ancestors; pink roses suggest tenderness, vulnerability, or compassion; and the exquisite green rose suggests the blossoming heart of nature.

Wilted Rose

A wilted rose may indicate that the relationship in question needs more nourishment to flourish. Consider whether this relationship is asking for more attention, time, presence, or energy in order to be healthy. Love, like roses, is resilient enough to weather storms and unintentional neglect and bounces back when given delicate care.

Thornbush

Don't be afraid if you envision a gnarly thornbush, which could indicate conflict, tension, or a dormant relationship. The thornbush points to those pain points where our humanity meets our divinity. Life on earth is challenging and messy when infinite spirit contracts to a single point in a physical body. Richard Katz, founder of the Flower Essence Society, shares a beautiful sentiment: "We often wonder why roses have thorns, but isn't it so wonderful that thornbushes have roses?"[12] What might this thorny relationship be trying to teach you about how to realize your spiritual potential? Everything blossoms in its own time.

Take a moment to reflect in your journal about your relationships and what your silent love chakra is trying to tell you.

---

12 Richard Katz, "12 Windows of Plant Perception," lecture presented at the Spirit Seed School: Ecological Consciousness & Reciprocity, June 2021.

CHAPTER SIX

SUMMARY

The awareness of breath is shared by all living things, now and forever. Use these silent love chakra practices to move beyond your regular day-to-day consciousness and engage with nature and the anima mundi.

7

SELF-HEALING AND GROUNDING

AMELIA VOGLER

This chapter dives into the relationship between your soul and your heart. Here you will ground yourself as a self-healer by expanding the core foundations of healing and awakening your fourth chakra's simple yet extraordinary potential through experiential practices.

A balanced heart chakra provides your soul an open pathway for growth and evolution, allowing the divine energies from above to inform the more earthly and body-based energies from below. An open, loving heart is required to align with self and nature.

I am a soul healer. I answer the fundamental questions about how to stay close to your inner light. I work with individuals to help them feel whole again, especially after they have shut down part of themselves. A healthy expression of love—the province of your heart chakra—is your compass as you navigate the path of wholeness and healing, and it places you in direct conversation with the beauty of life all around you.

FOUNDATIONS FOR SELF-HEALING

As with all chakra work, a good starting point is to release any desired outcomes. Allow your mind to be quiet and your heart will surely open. You will discover the silent love that expresses loudly through the heart chakra and even more loudly throughout your life.

Before you begin these practices, I'd like to present the possibility that everything you have been through in this lifetime or other lifetimes has fully prepared you to work in the subtle landscape of your heart chakra. Begin with this affirmation: *I am enough.*

PRACTICE

OPENING YOUR HEART CHAKRA

The heart chakra sits in the center of your chest and serves as a bridge between your lower, more earthly chakras and your upper, more spiritual chakras. This heart chakra bridge provides your soul an open pathway for growth and evolution, allowing the divine energies from above to inform the more earthly and body-based energies from below. An open, loving heart is required to align with self and nature. The word *spiritual* means many different things to different people, so connect with whatever this concept means to you and use that idea as you explore this chakra.

When your heart comes into balance, the bridge is built. Then you can allow the spiritual to inspire what is earthly and the earthly to ground what is spiritual.

Preparation

Find a quiet and welcoming space for this exercise. Bring paper and pen if you like to journal or process through writing. If you love color or art, gather paper and colored pencils. Employ any personal practices you have in your tool kit, such as deep breathing and mindful focus, to steady and clear your mind of chatter. If you have a naturally chatty mind, try extending your exhale longer than your inhale for a few cycles of breath.

Intention

This practice will balance the heart chakra's energies in order to connect with the energies of your soul essence and build a bridge to share your authenticity with the world.

Come to this practice with sincerity, making a simple and pure request from your heart on behalf of your heart. When healing the heart chakra, your power will come from connecting with your pure and inherent truth.

You may want to understand different aspects of your authenticity as you channel and connect to these energies. Knowing yourself is a noble inquiry, and this practice will help you channel the energies of your authentic self. Trust what you notice, and know that these personal energies support your unique balance.

Steps

» Sit or lie in any position that feels comfortable.

» Close your eyes or soften your gaze.

» Place your palms on your heart center and, by intention, access your fourth chakra and auric field.

» Sincerely ask Creator or Spirit to bring forth your authentic self's unique and personal energies to open and balance your fourth chakra. These energies will transform any inauthentic energies from your past into those that naturally express your true self.

» Intentionally receive these unique and personal energies. Take notes, journal, or draw to help you process any shifts.

» (Optional) After a bit of time has passed, gently call forth the energies of your heart and explore the healing energies that come with self-love and gentle curiosity. You can use these prompts or one of your own:

*What are the qualities of the energies
that opened your heart?*

Was there a color or colors that came through?

*What is an aspect of yourself that
you love and appreciate?*

What is one of your greatest strengths?

PRACTICE

GROUNDING YOUR HEART
WITH PERSONAL STAR ENERGY

When we work with energy and the soul, we use metaphoric language. In this practice you will call yourself forward from long ago through the metaphor of your original star.

Preparation

This star contains your core light essence and your most sincere truths. From an elemental perspective, the star reflects the alchemy of fire. This means that it can energetically purify, activate, and transform. It is also etheric, able to carry absolute truth and purity. According to the ancient

Greeks, ether was an element that most related to God and allowed humans to connect to their higher thoughts, intuition, and God's nature. In the Hindu tradition, the yogis attributed ether to connecting with one's highest possibilities and potential.

In this homing practice, you will ground your true essence, your personal star energy, into the center of your heart chakra. At first it might seem that you will be bringing this energy from beyond yourself, as if considering the stars beyond you in the cosmos, but you are actually summoning forth energies from deep within, from long ago, from your original code. These energies stream to you from within through the center of your heart chakra and the origin of your being. Your essence is coded in the light of your original star. Now it is time to call the star of yourself home.

Intention

This practice will ground yourself in the light you are, the light you have been, and the light you will always be.

Steps

> » Sit quietly in meditation or intentional thought and sincerely connect with your unique star.

> » Feel, sense, and experience that star as if looking at it from beyond.

» Introduce yourself as if you are meeting a few friends with whom you feel instantly safe. This introduction need not be verbalized; it is an intentional opening.

» Notice how the door to your heart opens and the lotus leaves related to it shimmer. You can also relate to the celestial wishing tree you activated in chapter 1 and interact with it as well. Breathe in your starlight.

» Allow your heart to open to this relationship. Be patient in this step as your heart opens to the entirety of your essence. You will first notice that the energies flow quickly, but as your heart chakra begins to integrate, you will notice that a portal or an open space appears.

» Call forth the energy of your original star and allow your star energy to fill the open space.

» Give yourself room for the bigness of who you are to be welcomed into this space.

Receiving love is one of the most remarkable medicines of the heart chakra, and welcoming your own essence is a transformative first step in grounding the energies of the heart chakra and expanding your potential for self-love.

PRACTICE

ENERGIZING THE POTENTIAL
OF THE HEART CHAKRA

The heart is a relational chakra. It gives and receives. It breathes in goodness and exhales goodness in return. In this practice you will awaken the potential of the heart chakra by sending love to those who are suffering.

Lynne McTaggart, an award-winning journalist, international best-selling author, and one of my mentors, studies the power of healing intention. One of the most important aspects of her research suggests the power of "getting over yourself," or offering healing in the service of others.

Being in service to others is like gourmet food for feeding the heart chakra because you connect to your heart's greatest desire, which is to be of service and make a difference.

You may think this outward expression of energy will be draining, but in fact, as Lynne's research has confirmed, this sharing of love and healing returns the energy back to those who take the time to give love to others.

Preparation

Name someone who is suffering or a group of people who are. It isn't hard to look into the world and find an individual or group needing additional support. If no one comes to mind, you can use an open intention of sending your heart energies generally to those who are suffering.

Intention

This practice will share your heart's energy with those who are suffering.

Steps

» Sit quietly in meditation or intentional thought and sincerely connect with a person, a group of people, or any living thing needing healing. (Of course, our beautiful planet, Mother Earth, can be included.)

» Place your hands on your heart and connect with your heart chakra energy.

» Send energy from your heart into your hands so that your hands fill with that energy.

» Allow your hands to be moved beyond your heart by this energy, opening them slowly, palms facing outward.

» By intention, allow your heart energy to flow through your heart, arms, and palms to the beings to whom you are sending this love and caring.

SUMMARY

The fourth chakra is the bridge between the spiritual and the earthly and brings your highest service into reality. Consider that your highest service is to be for something larger than yourself. Manifesting this requires both your inspiration from the Divine (the power, the vision, the expression) and the groundedness of your body (the physical, emotional, and will force). You have fueled your purpose with self-love and expansion through opening, balancing, supporting, and energizing your heart chakra.

8

GUIDED MEDITATIONS

AMANDA HUGGINS

When we connect to the heart chakra through meditation, we're tapping into the essence of universal energy: love. Meditation is an age-old way to create the reality of love through our subtle energetics.

In our world, the concept of love is often misconstrued as something that can be given, taken away, or restricted based on conditions. Often the misconceptions about love being a finite resource have arisen from experiences of conditional love or attachments (heartbreak, pain, even trauma) that have left us feeling vulnerable and fearful of losing the love we hold dear. When we attach ourselves to narratives that depict love as scarce or limited, we inadvertently create barriers that close off our heart chakra. As we buy into these stories, we block the free flow of love's energy within us and inhibit our ability to experience its fullness.

Yet the essence of love is infinite and boundless and transcends all human limitations. It is an energy that emanates from the core of our being, and when we connect with the heart chakra through meditation, we're able to tap back into this boundless wellspring of love. As we sit in quiet contemplation, our breath becomes a guiding rhythm, leading us deeper into the heart space. With each inhalation and exhalation, we are reminded of the constant flow of life force energy that sustains us. In this process, the heart chakra becomes a nexus of loving energy, radiating warmth, compassion, and acceptance through us and beyond.

THE HEART CHAKRA AND EMOTIONAL HEALING

It's not unusual for folks to experience some resistance to working with the heart chakra, as it requires acknowledging, embracing, and releasing past emotional wounds and traumas. We've been taught to label some emotions—such as anger, sadness, or pain—as negative or undesirable, while promoting others—like joy, gratitude, or creativity—as positive. This categorization leads us to suppress emotions that are perceived as negative, which only perpetuates inner discord and prevents holistic healing.

If you're afraid of the emotions that might come forward when you connect with your heart, keep this in mind:

all emotions are created equal. In our complex human experience, emotions are like colors on the vast tapestry of life, each contributing to the richness and depth of our experience. Honoring all your emotions in meditation is an act of radical self-acceptance and self-love. It's a beautiful paradox: the act of fully experiencing your emotions, even the uncomfortable ones, is what allows the process of healing to unfold.

My favorite mantra, "Feel it to heal it," encapsulates this principle. Instead of avoiding or suppressing emotions, allow yourself to truly feel them in a safe and nurturing space. When you create this container within your heart chakra meditation, you're granting yourself permission to unravel the layers of emotional energy that have been held within you. Just as a wound needs to be cleaned and tended to before it can heal, your emotions need to be acknowledged and felt to facilitate true healing. The heart chakra serves as a space where emotional pain can be acknowledged, processed, and ultimately healed. By meditating on the heart chakra, you're lovingly engaging in your heart's healing.

A PATHWAY TO SELF-LOVE

Meditating with the heart chakra is a powerful pathway for cultivating a deeper sense of compassion toward yourself. Practicing self-love through heart chakra meditations is especially important for people pleasers and those who tend to put themselves last. In our busy lives, it's all too common to neglect self-care and self-kindness; we may extend love and compassion to others effortlessly yet struggle to offer the same level of care to ourselves. Heart-centered meditations gently guide you to redirect this universal love toward your own being. As you focus on the heart chakra, you're creating a sacred space within your inner landscape where self-love can flourish.

Connecting with the heart sends a powerful message to the subconscious mind. You are deserving of love, kindness, and acceptance just as you are. This process isn't about seeking perfection or achieving a flawless state of enlightenment. Rather, it's about nurturing a genuine, unconditional love for yourself, even during moments of vulnerability and imperfection. Through this practice you're also dissolving the barriers that may have hindered your connection to self-love. Past experiences, societal expectations, and self-critical thoughts can build walls around your heart, making it difficult to truly embrace yourself. Meditating with the heart chakra helps dismantle these barriers brick by brick, offering a safe space for your true essence to shine through.

LOVING-KINDNESS MEDITATION

To begin, find a quiet and comfortable space where you won't be disturbed. Sit down, relax your body, and close your eyes. Allow any tension to melt away as you settle into this moment of self-care and inner connection.

Place a hand on your heart for the first few breaths as you ground into your body. Feel the warmth of your hands against your heart and the gentle rising and falling of your chest against your palm, and notice the subtle feeling of your heartbeat. As you inhale, imagine you're drawing in love, light, and compassion. As you exhale, release any tension, negativity, or self-doubt.

Silently repeat to yourself:

May my heart be open. May I be filled with
love and compassion. May I extend kindness
to myself and others always, in all ways.

Bring your awareness to your heart chakra. Visualize a soft, radiant light in the center of your chest, and see that light gently expanding with each breath. You may visualize this light as green or perhaps you see it as another healing color. Trust your intuition; whatever color you see is exactly the color and vibration that's needed for your practice.

Imagine that this healing light represents pure love and kindness. Allow your body to match that energetic vibration. With each inhalation, feel that light growing brighter and more vibrant.

Turn your attention to the exhalations. With each one, repeat the following phrases to yourself, either silently or aloud.

May I be happy.

May I be healthy.

May I be safe.

May I live with ease.

Feel the energy of these words vibrating at the center of your heart. See that energy pouring out from the center of your being and filling up your entire auric field. Envision this warmth of love enveloping you.

Now bring to mind someone you care about deeply. As you hold their image, repeat the same phrases, substituting "I" with "you."

May you be happy.

May you be healthy.

May you be safe.

May you live with ease.

Extend your loving-kindness to them, sending waves of compassion from your heart to theirs.

See your cocoon of compassion expanding to encapsulate this person.

Gradually expand this cocoon of loving-kindness to include others in your life: family, friends, colleagues, and even those you have challenges with. Repeat the phrases for each person, allowing your heart chakra to radiate love and healing energy.

Finally, expand your loving-kindness to encompass all beings everywhere. Picture the entire world bathed in the light of your heart chakra, and repeat those same four phrases again.

To close the meditation, gently release the phrases and the visualization. Gradually become aware of your physical body, the sensation of your breath, and the space around you.

As you open your eyes, take a moment to thank yourself for dedicating this time to nourishing your heart and soul. Whenever you're ready to move on with your day, do your best to carry this energy of love and kindness with you.

"FEEL IT TO HEAL IT" MEDITATION

Find a comfortable and quiet space to lie down. Allow your body to be supported by a bed, cushions, or blankets underneath you so you can fully surrender your body weight and relax. Bring your hands to your heart and close your eyes.

Feel the warmth of your hands on your chest and begin to connect with the heart chakra.

Bring awareness to your breath. Feel the gentle rising and falling of your chest against your palms as you inhale and exhale.

Begin tuning in to any emotions that are present within you. As you notice emotions arising, call them out without identifying yourself as those emotions. For example, *I am feeling sadness* or *I am feeling anger* rather than *I am sad* or *I am angry*. This slight phrasing adjustment, though subtle, empowers you to recognize that these emotions are temporary experiences passing through your awareness.

Whatever emotions arise, allow yourself to acknowledge them without judgment. Whether it's sadness, anger, joy, or anything in between, give yourself permission to feel without suppressing or avoiding.

If shadow emotions arise, the mind may want to fix or problem-solve them. Be mindful of this. Instead, simply allow the emotions to be witnessed without trying to fix or change them. This is the practice of emotional validation: gently granting yourself permission to experience your emotions without judgment or the need for immediate resolution.

When shadow emotions surface, it's often because they are seeking acknowledgment and release. By allowing yourself to witness them without attaching judgment or criticism, you create a nurturing environment in which these emotions can be heard and understood. Just as you would hold space for a friend sharing their feelings, you offer the same compassionate attention to your own emotions. This approach facilitates a gentle unfolding of emotions and encourages a deeper understanding of their origins and their impact on your well-being.

As the emotions unfold, imagine that each breath you take is like a soothing balm gently embracing and releasing any emotional tension.

Breathe. Be with these emotions. If tears want to flow or if anger wants to arise, allow that to happen as you continue to witness and validate the emotions you are experiencing. You may also choose to speak directly to the emotion. For instance, *I see and honor you, sadness. I am here with you.*

Imagine that with each inhale, you're drawing fresh energy and light into your heart chakra. As you exhale, release any emotional heaviness or stagnation. Picture this energy flowing through your heart chakra, creating a sense of spaciousness and renewal.

Now bring your attention back to the soft light in your heart chakra. As you breathe, silently recite this mantra:

> *All of my emotions are valid,*
> *and I release what no longer serves me.*

Allow your heart space to fill with a sense of self-love and acceptance. As you breathe, focus on feelings of gratitude for yourself and for this time of self-care and emotional exploration.

Slowly bring your awareness back to your physical surroundings. Wiggle your fingers and toes, allowing yourself to return to the present moment.

As you go about your day, remember this practice of feeling it to heal it. Allow yourself to experience and release emotions, knowing that by doing so you're creating space for healing and transformation. With an open heart, you can continue to cultivate love, compassion, and emotional well-being within yourself and the world around you.

PRACTICE

MEDITATION FOR RECEIVING THE
ENDLESS FLOW OF UNIVERSAL LOVE

Find a comfortable seat where you are gently relaxed while keeping your spine supported. Close your eyes and take a few deep, calming breaths to settle into the present moment.

Begin by bringing your awareness to your breath. Inhale deeply through your nose, allowing your abdomen to expand. Exhale slowly through your mouth, releasing any tension or stress. With each breath, feel yourself becoming more grounded and at ease. If you notice any resistance in your body or heart space, simply draw your attention to that part of your body and use the breath to release any tension there.

Visualize yourself surrounded by a vast, radiant field of golden light. Imagine that this light is filled with the boundless, infinite love that exists within the universe.

See this field of light enveloping you completely, embracing you in its warmth and compassion. As you do, feel into the vibrations of love, compassion, and healing. Invite a sense of warmth and comfort into the body.

With each inhalation, imagine that you're drawing in this golden light through the crown of your head and into your entire body. As you exhale, release any tension or negativity, allowing it to dissolve into the light. This is a practice in receiving; notice whether there is resistance to the simplicity of just receiving love. If any resistance occurs, offer yourself this affirmation: *I am worthy of receiving love.*

Shift your attention to your heart space. Visualize your heart chakra as a radiant, glowing sphere of energy. Feel the warmth and gentle pulsations emanating from this area.

Imagine that the golden light of universal love begins to pour directly into your heart chakra. With each breath, this light expands and fills your heart space. Visualize this light cleansing away any pain, resistance, heartbreak, or other blockages that prevent you from receiving this unconditional love.

Grounded in your heart center and feeling the vibration of unconditional love, recite the following affirmations to yourself, allowing each one to resonate deeply within you.

I am a vessel of universal love.

*I am connected to the infinite stream of
love that flows through all existence.*

I am worthy of receiving and sharing boundless love.

*My heart is open to giving and
receiving love in its purest form.*

Visualize your heart chakra glowing even brighter, radiating the golden light of universal love outward. Imagine this light reaching out to touch the hearts of everyone around you, regardless of time and space. Picture it bridging gaps, fostering connection, and igniting a sense of oneness.

As you sit in this radiant space of love, allow yourself to simply be. Receive the flow of universal love circulating within you, nourishing your body, mind, and spirit. Embrace the sensation of being completely held and supported by this divine energy. Trust that there is nothing for you to "do" except be.

When you're ready to close the meditation, take a few moments to express gratitude for the experience of connecting with universal love. Gently bring your awareness back to your physical surroundings, wiggling your fingers and toes. When you're ready, open your eyes.

SUMMARY

Remember that the boundless love you've tapped into is always available to you whenever you need to connect, heal, and share. By cultivating this connection with universal love, you are aligning with the very essence of the heart chakra. Meditation is a perfect activity for linking your own heart space with the creative and unconditional love that is available universally.

9

VIBRATIONAL REMEDIES

JO-ANNE BROWN

When life is turbulent and the people who have been main-stays in our lives are no longer there for us, other individuals show up. In my time of need, amazing individuals assisted me, and I was also fortified by vibrational remedies that revitalized my heart chakra energies. Vibrational remedies can be truly beneficial, and I am confident they can do the same for you.

These remedies are intended to aid you with the most challenging of heart chakra problems. Often the most devastating and crushing experiences of the heart involve relationships, especially the endings of them and the subsequent loss of connection through separation or death. While writing this chapter, I experienced both. My marriage of seventeen years crumbled, and my mother's health steadily declined. While I was able to spend precious time with my mother before she passed away, I was also separated from my former husband, my beloved fur babies, and my local support network.

In this chapter I share my understanding of vibrational remedies for the fourth chakra. I will cover my preferred practice-based and tangible remedies, explain their usage, describe their benefits, and outline two practices to help you support your fourth chakra anytime and anywhere.

WHAT ARE VIBRATIONAL REMEDIES?

Vibrational remedies are practices and medicines that enable natural balance and flow. When the fourth chakra isn't healthy, we tend to respond to life in one of two ways: by becoming hardhearted, self-centered, and unlovable or by self-sacrificing and people-pleasing. When we experience vibrational remedies specifically crafted for the fourth chakra, our equilibrium is restored, allowing us to be loving, empathetic, and respectful of our own needs as well as the needs of others.

WHAT IS RESONANCE?

Resonance is a physical phenomenon that occurs when an object vibrates at its preferred or natural frequency and its vibration achieves maximum strength, or amplitude.

As physical beings, we experience resonance through our chakras and our physical bodies. One physical form of this is heart resonance, or heart coherence: a natural state where our body's systems are in sync with one another. This produces an optimal state of homeostasis, or balance, that also stabilizes us mentally, emotionally, and spiritually.

In the same way, when our silent love chakra is exposed to the self-regulating energies of vibrational remedies, we synchronize with those supportive energies and they produce positive change.

THE INFLUENCE OF THE HEART CHAKRA

In part 1 Cyndi called the heart chakra "the center of your own universe." She also made clear that the heart produces the strongest rhythmic field produced in the human body. Cyndi's exercise literally described what happens vibrationally since the heart's magnetic field is the strongest rhythmic field produced in the human body.

This directly aligns with how traditional Chinese medicine (TCM) views the heart: as the king or emperor, the most influential of our physical organs, governing the blood and all our internal organs.

Our heart chakras are radiant centers of love that give us the capacity to love ourselves and others.

Within our bodies, the vibrations of our heart's magnetic field communicate self-love through our thymus gland, resulting in a cellular response that leads to good physical immunity.

We also influence people and social groups around us through our heart's field as we transmit our personal loving beliefs and attitudes beyond our physical boundaries.

VIBRATIONAL REMEDIES FOR YOUR FOURTH CHAKRA

Vibrational remedies fall into one of two categories:

- » practice-based remedies
- » tangible remedies

Practice-Based Vibrational Remedies

These include subtle energy treatments, therapies, and practices that can sometimes require the guidance of a qualified practitioner. They support our fourth/silent love chakra energies through:

- » direct skin contact (including grounding, kinesiology, acupuncture, and massage)
- » vibrational media (including sound therapies, frequency-based modalities, and qigong)
- » demonstrational guidance (including yoga)

I have found that the benefits of the direct skin contact remedies range widely because they are so personal to each person's body.

I will now highlight in greater detail four modalities that are extremely effective for heart chakra support.

The first two of these methods—grounding and kinesiology—work through direct skin contact, and the other two methods are vibrational media: sound therapies and frequency-based modalities.

> **GROUNDING.** This ancient practice requires direct contact with the earth. It connects us to a layer of free electrons on the earth's surface that balances our electrical circuitry and blood pressure by discharging stress and counteracting degenerative processes, such as inflammatory heart disease. Research shows that grounding also improves blood circulation and flow, aids in wound healing, and improves the effects of inflammatory processes overall.[13] A healthier and happier cardiovascular system and heart produces a happier you at every level.

13 James L. Oschman et al., "The Effects of Grounding (Earthing) on Inflammation, the Immune Response, Wound Healing, and Prevention and Treatment of Chronic Inflammatory and Autoimmune Diseases," *Journal of Inflammation Research* 8 (March 24, 2015): 83–96, https://doi .org/10.2147/JIR.S69656.

In this practice the earth becomes our practitioner. However, rather than having skin-to-skin contact with a human practitioner, we are grounded through direct skin-to-earth contact with our natural environment. Grounding occurs naturally when we are involved in activities such as walking barefoot on grass, dirt, or sand; gardening; climbing a tree; connecting with our pets or other animals; and eating root vegetables.

When you don't have access to the natural environment, a vast array of grounding tools are also readily available, including grounding bed linens, blankets, clothing, and shoes. Grounding mats can be particularly beneficial, and many come with interwoven gemstones and use various bands of infrared, which can reduce inflammation.

PRACTICE

GROUNDING FOR THE HEART CHAKRA

Find space in a natural environment where you can safely stand (preferably barefoot), sit, or lie down without being disturbed.

Take a moment to gently massage the skin on each side of the fingernail on both of your little fingers. In doing this you are stimulating your heart meridian as described in TCM and, by extension, your heart chakra.

Take a few deep breaths in and out, and allow yourself to relax.

Place your open hands palms down on the earth's surface and focus on your little fingers. Visualize the flow of life-supporting electrons emanating from the earth as they make connections with your hands and your little fingers. Know that this natural interaction is supporting your heart and your heart chakra. Stay in this space for as long as you choose.

KINESIOLOGY. Aristotle first coined the word *kinesiology* back in 300 BCE to describe the movement of the physical body. In the 1960s Dr. George Goodheart built on Aristotle's work when he developed the practice of applied kinesiology, which uses manual muscle-strength testing to identify and correct imbalances in the human body.

This modality also detects chakra imbalances through the meridians associated with each chakra. For the heart chakra, these meridians include the heart and circulation / sex meridians.

In a session, qualified kinesiologists access subconscious connections and unlock past experiences and events that have caused heart chakra blockages and disharmony.

SOUND THERAPIES. Research has shown that supportive frequencies for the fourth chakra are in the range of 349 Hz to 440 Hz. I frequently work with 417 Hz, one of three solfeggio frequencies that relate to numerology's earth or physical plane. The other two are 174 Hz and 741 Hz.

Another of my preferred frequencies to balance the heart chakra is 528 Hz, which is often described as the "love frequency."

FREQUENCY-BASED THERAPIES. These therapies employ the use of low-voltage frequency-generating devices, such as the Rife machine, and conductive electrodes to send beneficial vibrations to the body to address causative factors of dis-ease and ill health.

Optimal resonating vibrations are chosen to support the heart chakra and its corresponding organs and meridians as described in TCM. Due to the conductive nature of the meridians, as the vibrations are received, they energetically balance the targeted organs.

For example, blockages in the heart meridian can be released with 60 Hz and 3.7 kHz frequencies, and those in the lung meridian can be cleared with 10 Hz and 46 kHz frequencies.

Tangible Vibrational Remedies

These remedies are "medicines" that are stored in readily available carriers to allow quick absorption and integration within the human body. Typical carriers include water- and alcohol-based fluids, pills and pilules, oils, ointments, and salves. Essential oils influence us through our sense of smell and are commonly diffused in a water-based medium.

HOMEOPATHIC REMEDIES. Homeopathy is a type of alternative medicine that treats illnesses with minute doses of natural substances. During diagnosis, remedies are prescribed at appropriate potencies to produce a curative reaction in the patient without disturbing or damaging the body.

The silent love chakra has a more relational and spiritual focus than the lower three chakras, so accurately matching key heart chakra symptoms with an appropriate remedy is more complex. For this reason, it is recommended that remedies of this nature be prescribed by a qualified practitioner.

Homeopathic remedies that promote healthy fourth chakra energies include Aconitum napellus (for shock and for heart and lung support), Aurum metallicum (for blood pressure imbalances, pneumonia, and loneliness), Natrum muriaticum (for grief, heartache, and respiratory problems), and Ignatia amara (for grief, shock, and emotional sensitivity).[14]

FLOWER ESSENCES. This once-ancient healing modality was revived in the early 1900s when Dr. Edward Bach discovered that flower essences can rebalance physical and emotional disturbances within human subtle energy systems. While many high-integrity flower essences are available, here I'm featuring essences with heart chakra qualities and benefits I've personally experienced.

» *Bach flower remedies.* Dr. Edward Bach is the creator of the thirty-eight Bach flower remedies. Of these, my preferred remedies for the heart chakra include Beech (for compassion and tolerance), Chicory (for unconditional love), Vine (for acceptance of others), and Water Violet (for healthy connection).

---

14 These homeopathic remedies were sourced from qjure.com.

» *Elementals flower essence range*. Lindsay Fauntleroy, acupuncturist and author, developed this range of essences, describing them as self-awareness tools that introduce us to the higher truths of our souls. (Lindsay also wrote chapter 6 of this book, on embodying fourth chakra wisdom.) Two essences in her range series are particularly supportive of the heart chakra: Wholehearted (for compassion, courage, and healthy connection) and Open (for openness, trust, and vulnerability in relationships). My personal recommendation is the Wholehearted essence blend. It was one of the remedies that emotionally sustained me during the ending of my marriage and my mother's transition from the earthly plane.

» *Australian bushflower essences*. This extensive range of individual and blended flower-based remedies was created by Ian White, an Australian herbalist. Ian describes these remedies as catalysts to unlock your full potential, resolve negative beliefs, and create emotional health and well-being. My preferred remedies from this range for the fourth chakra include Relationship Essence (for healthy connection), Bluebell (for openheartedness and unconditional love), Flannel Flower (for openness, trust, and expression of feelings), and

Carer's Essence (for inner strength, resilience, and self-care).

Following are two vibrational practices to support your heart chakra.

PRACTICE

HEALING SOUNDS FOR THE HEART CHAKRA

Sound therapy is an ancient form of vibrational healing. The six healing sounds (*Liu Zi Jue*) from qigong are a sound therapy practice that has been used for centuries to promote chi (or energy) and create resonance in our bodies through a six-part breathing practice. This requires the air to be drawn in through the nose and slowly released through the mouth. In this practice, we will work with the healing sounds that create resonance in the fourth chakra yin organs, specifically in the heart and the lungs.

For the Heart

» Take three deep breaths in and out, and then place your left hand on your heart chakra.

» Breathe in and visualize red (the color that represents the heart in TCM).

» Breathe out the heart healing sound, pronounced *Haaaaa*. Visualize this outward breath as coming from your heart or your heart chakra.

» Breathe out and visualize the unhealthy energies of indifference, hardheartedness, and lack of forgiveness being released from your heart. As you breathe in, visualize those energies being replaced with love, healing, and joy.

For the Lungs

» Take three deep breaths in and out, and then place your left hand on your heart chakra.

» Breathe in and visualize the color white (this represents the lungs in TCM).

» Breathe out the lung healing sound, pronounced *Sssss*. Visualize this outward breath as coming from your lungs, on both sides of your heart chakra.

» Breathe out and visualize the unhealthy energies of unresolved grief and paralyzing sorrow being released from your lungs. As you breathe in, visualize those energies being replaced with courage and the ability to face the future.

SUMMARY

Through beautiful heart-based vibrational remedies, we can balance self-love with love for others and find healing in a most harmonious and peaceful way.

This chapter included several remedies and practices to support all aspects of your loving and empathetic anahata chakra. Now sit back and see what happens as you send out your unique love frequencies from your heart chakra into the world.

10

CRYSTALS, MINERALS, AND STONES

MARGARET ANN LEMBO

Selecting gemstones to support your fourth chakra is not only a fruitful activity but an enjoyable one too. Your best choices will reinforce the core purpose of the heart chakra: to nurture love.

When you focus on your heart chakra, you recognize that your true essence is love—that you are love. The stones I'll cover in this chapter will help you become more loving in all that you do, say, think, feel, smell, taste, and know.

The primary color of this fourth/silent love chakra is green, so you'll mainly want to select green stones to enable a healthy chakra. The secondary color I work with for this chakra is pink. The vibration of pink at the heart is the blended energy of red from the root chakra and white from the crown chakra. So choose pink or green gemstones to rebalance and align your heart center. That will help you recalibrate this chakra with the crystal-clear intention to vibrate at "the rate of love."

RELATIONSHIPS ARE EVERYWHERE

Whatever you focus on becomes your reality, so it's important to hold a focus on what you want to experience in life. This is especially true of relationships. We are in relationship with everything, down to the minutiae of our lives. It is obvious when we are in relationships with other people, but, for many of us, the relationship we have with ourselves is less clear.

Our connections with others are of many types and levels, including those with friends, neighbors, acquaintances, coworkers, employees, supervisors, authority figures, family, extended family, and more. Additionally, relationships exist between us and nature in all its forms—with the animals in our lives, for instance—and even between ourselves and inanimate objects, such as cars, computers, TVs, and other objects.

The connection with ourselves is just as layered as all our other relationships, but conscious intention is often required to bring it to our awareness.

CRYSTALS, MINERALS, AND STONES

INTENTION

Setting an intention is central to working with gemstones for chakra balancing and healing. To choose the perfect stone to match your intention, focus on the image or thought of your intention and then look at the choices of crystals that are available to you, either at a store or from your own collection. Here I'll provide my recommendations for which stones to use, but if you are drawn to a gemstone, go with your gut and what you find attractive. Match your positive thought with that gemstone and watch your world realign into what you have decided you want to create.

When a gemstone is paired with a daily affirmation, the stone amplifies that intention, so I have included sample affirmations in the discussions of individual stones that follow.

LIVING AND LOVING UNCONDITIONALLY USING GEMSTONES

Loving yourself unconditionally is the first step toward awakening your heart center. To stimulate your heart center, get to know yourself better, honor yourself more fully, and spend enjoyable quality time with yourself.

Living unconditionally and loving unconditionally are very similar. Remember that when you truly love someone, you don't withhold your love because they aren't behaving as you want them to or as society dictates. It may be that the way they express love is simply different from how you do.

Here are some of my favorite gemstones to enable pure, unconditional love:

Calcite supports you during a change of heart. There are both green and pink varieties, and both are effective. This is a very nurturing stone for your heart center during a change in relationship such as marriage or divorce, or changes in any other relationship, including those at work. With calcite, you can use affirmations such as these: *Even in a changing world, I feel steady and secure. Kindness and thoughtfulness are part of my nature. I enjoy loving relationships.*

Kunzite is a reminder that love is the answer to all. Use this stone to radiate love in a wide circumference around your being. Remember that since the heart chakra is the center of your consciousness, love is who you truly are. Kunzite makes this easier by helping you maintain focus and attention on your heart chakra and on love. With this gem in hand, telepathically transmit loving thoughts to people, places, and things to make this world a better place. This stone is ideal to use in circumstances where there are discordant words and thoughts, helping transform and transmute them into harmonious interactions. Affirmations such as the following will especially bolster kunzite's power: *I am so grateful that I am happy! I feel comfort. I know I am blessed. I radiate love and attract love.*

Rose quartz activates the heart chakra as the bridge between the upper three and lower three chakras. This is significant because this bridge helps connect your human existence as a grounded individual on this planet with your spiritual life. Rose quartz aligns your consciousness with divine love, compassion, mercy, tolerance, and kindness. Make your own affirmations for the pink splendor of rose quartz or try this: *I acknowledge, accept, and respect differing belief systems.*

CONSCIOUS RELATIONSHIP

As you develop spiritually, you enter relationships with more conscious awareness. A conscious relationship means looking at yourself from many standpoints and being authentically present in the relationship. Because of our previous experiences with relationships, good and bad, it often takes great courage to move beyond hurt or fear of failure and into a new relationship. Stones can help.

As we covered earlier, your heart chakra stones can be any pink or green gem. Here are a few for when you are working on being in a conscious relationship; I have also added a clear stone.

Danburite, a stone of harmony and beneficial relation-ships, is an excellent tool for connecting with higher-level spiritual love. Danburite empowers you to connect with your highest vibration, aligning you with your divine pur-pose and sacred heart. Gaze into danburite to imagine and manifest spiritually aligned relationships. This stone helps you maintain a cooperative attitude to create an atmo-sphere of happiness and offers energy to help you forge valuable friendships, love relationships, or even a solid mar-riage. Invite the vibration of danburite with these affirma-tions: *I radiate light and love. I emanate a harmonious vibration, and people feel peaceful around me. I am blessed with a fantastic significant other, presently known or unknown. I have amazing friends.*

Ruby in fuchsite vibrates with the energy of spiritu-ally aligned romantic love. The soft green vibration of the fuchsite gently prods you toward accepting friend-ships and relationships, while the brilliant ruby energizes you to embrace relationships with open arms. Try a more outgoing outlook, and be willing to connect. Think about getting back into a romantic relationship or rekindling an existing one. Embrace your personal power, recognize your magnificence, and enjoy fulfilling interactions with others. Affirmations can include the following: *I am very loving. My* *friends, companions, and colleagues are the best in so many ways. I love to share my love and my life with others.*

Tabular clear quartz is easily identified by shape, as two sides of the crystal are much wider than the other four sides. Flat and tablet-like, it easily transmits the language of light with the conscious intent of the user. Often called tabbies, these quartz crystals are good for communication, including telepathic linking, or heart-to-heart and mind-to-mind communication. Tabbies are the marriage counselors of the gemstone kingdom because they help you actively engage in good communication, and the key to any good relationship is the ability to communicate well and truly listen. You can relax into the relationship when you know you are being heard and can speak your truth. Use affirmations like the following to pull forward what this stone offers: *I am heard and understood. When I express myself, I fluently visualize and send mental pictures. I communicate from my heart to all other hearts.*

HEART-CENTERED EMOTIONAL BALANCE AND HEALING

As you gain a deeper understanding of each of the chakras, you also develop a deeper understanding of people and their emotional challenges, as well as your own. This intimate look into each aspect of human nature offers you the opportunity to stop judging yourself and others. As you open your heart, you can allow judgment to give way to simple observation.

Feelings are manifestations of emotions, aspects of our human consciousness that result from sentiments and desires. They are emotional states that include awareness, impressions, and intuition, and they encompass higher emotions such as sensitivity and sensibility.

Emotions arise spontaneously without conscious effort. Suddenly, an emotion that you never saw coming—joy, sorrow, love, or dislike, for example—bubbles up from within and surprises you and everyone around you. The following stones can help foster heart-centered acceptance of whatever feelings arise.

Chrysoprase is a heart chakra stone you can use to open your heart to give love and, even more important, to let yourself receive love. Chrysoprase heightens your compassion for yourself when you realize that your repetitive thoughts are attracting unwanted situations. A member of the chalcedony family, it is an apple green or a seafoam green color. Because of the soothing energy of the green shades of chrysoprase, you may use it as a healing salve to ease a broken heart. This stone is useful when you are feeling emotionally vulnerable. Lovely affirmations for this stone are as follows: *Everything is going well. I have an open heart. I allow love and am very loving. I am nurtured and nurturing.*

Rhodochrosite is a peachy-pink to rosy-red stone that brings energy from the heart to the navel, bridging the two chakra centers. The challenges and buried emotions stored within the navel need love. It is quite simple: the key to restoring balance is to instill more love where there is pain, heartache, or angst, and rhodochrosite provides a bridge to love. Open your heart to release prior feelings of hurt or fear while employing affirmations like the following: *I am loving and balanced on all levels. I have the courage to fulfill my life's purpose.*

Rhodonite helps restore balance to your emotional body after a period of grief following a loss or disappointment. When you're going through emotional balancing or grief recovery, this stone reminds you that it's important to take the time you need to recover. This rosy gem helps you connect your heart and your mind and offers grounded support during times of heartache and sorrow. Draw from the following types of affirmations to support yourself: *I am always restoring and healing my body. I feel nourished and fulfilled.*

PRACTICE

DRINKING IN THE COLORS
OF THE HEART CHAKRA

Imagine you have the colors green and pink swirling around you. Inside the swirls are people you love and those who love you. Also present is the energy of good friends and nature. Imagine allowing all those good feelings to surround you, like your favorite blanket and pillow. Know that you are loved.

SUMMARY

Focusing on love in all you do, say, and think is essential to a healthy fourth chakra. Your loving thoughts, words, and actions will strengthen kindness and compassion for yourself and those around you. Use the gems covered in this chapter whenever you need to remember that your true essence is love. It is essential to use them with intention and focus on the positive so that your life reflects your highest potential. Let these gems guide you to improve your demeanor and attract new friends or a romantic partner. Remember that you create your life through your thoughts, actions, words, and deeds. Your intentions vibrate into the world and return to you in the form of your reality. Let crystals, minerals, and stones help you hold the vision of emitting love, kindness, and tolerance with your openhearted fourth chakra.

11

MANTRA HEALING

BLAKE TEDDER

When I was in my early twenties, I stumbled upon yoga and a wise teacher who introduced me to the healing power of sacred words called mantras—and everything changed. In this chapter I'm going to show you how to access the beautiful medicine of mantras. Mantras can improve any area of your life, but they are especially resonant when employed for your heart chakra, which yearns for relationship and connection. I'll reveal how these powerful vibrational tools can be used to reveal love and promote healing through your heart chakra. I will also provide practices to induce a clear, fresh state of heart openness to better all levels of your life.

First I want to briefly share what a difference mantra made in my life. Until I was introduced to yoga and mantra, I had legitimate reasons for curling up and shutting out the world. Six years earlier, I had survived a fiery plane crash in the mountains of Colorado. I underwent intense trauma, with burns on 35 percent of my body. Recovery included twelve major surgeries and a three-month touch-and-go stint in a hospital ICU. I was left with profound post-traumatic stress disorder (PTSD). The extreme anxiety, disassociation, anger, loneliness, and social alienation were intractable.

My teacher's guidance took me through deep experience with mantras and weekly kirtans, which are the call-and-response devotional chanting of mantras. My heart began to bloom. I started to understand how to accept and even love my life and experience joys and relationships I did not think possible. Mantra reduced my sense of alienation and allowed genuineness and vulnerability with others. I followed my expanding heart chakra and amplified its growing love for mantra and kirtan by going on to produce an internationally acclaimed kirtan radio show. I lived and breathed mantra music, even leading kirtan groups myself. I knew I had finally found a reliable tool to counteract the constricting forces of PTSD. What a gift.

WHAT IS A MANTRA?

Mantras are powerful vibrational and symbolic tools that can be chanted, sung, and meditated upon to affect your energy system. The word *mantra* is a Sanskrit word combining *manas* or "the thinking mind" and *trā*, or "instrument/tool." My favorite term for it is "mind protector"—a vehicle to help focus the mind and ward off the distractions and negative thinking we have all become accustomed to.

There are many kinds of mantras found in Hinduism, Buddhism, and Sikhism. Most have their roots in Sanskrit, the spiritual language of ancient India. Much different from how letters work in English, the building blocks of Sanskrit are spiritually significant vibratory sounds designed to resonate with specific parts of our subtle bodies and our chakras.

Traditional mantras are sacred words, phrases, formulas, and, in some traditions, the names of deities. Many are linked with ancient stories and proper pronunciation protocols that go back thousands of years. For someone with the understanding of these elements, working with mantras is extremely potent. Even without a deep understanding, we can receive many benefits from chanting mantras sincerely and to the best of our ability, especially if we hold faith in their medicine.

MANTRAS AND THE
POWER OF THOUGHTS

Recall a time when your heart spontaneously compelled you to do something caring for someone else but your fears and preoccupations pulled you back. This sometimes happens to me when I walk past someone begging on the street. I dispassionately look away while my heart screams at me to stop and connect with this fellow human being. My mind tells me familiar stories, such as "I'm already late" or "He'll use my money for drugs." But if I am honest with myself, my mind is simply unwilling to confront the shame I would feel if I truly witnessed the incongruity between our lives. My heart chakra, on the other hand, has no such concern. It wants to connect and heal.

Keeping us in relative physical and psychological safety is the mind's first job. Former experiences are overlaid on the present like a veil, limiting what we experience to protect us from our own fear and psychological pain. Of course, it is smart to be frightened of physical danger, but the mind can also go overboard, covering the heart chakra with anxieties and strategies to avoid upsetting the status quo. Mantras can disrupt this habitual patterning.

When we intone ancient mantras from Sanskrit or other spiritual languages, we directly manipulate the mental patterning in our energy systems with their spiritual and vibratory essences. These subtle mechanisms are advanced and beyond my understanding; however, I have faith in their power after reliably experiencing their effects as well as recognizing their remarkable durability through history. Thousands of generations of ancestors have carried forward these sacred phrases to the present. There must be something powerful going on.

PRACTICE

START SIMPLY WITH THE ESSENCE

Because the heart chakra is located in the chest, which is a resonating chamber for the human voice, chanting and singing mantras are ideal practices for breaking up thought patterns that prevent us from expressing love and connection. This first practice is a simple way to experience this effect.

Each chakra has an associated vocal sound in Sanskrit that you can use as a tool for activating and balancing it. When intoned, these seed syllables, or bija mantras, act like vibrational seeds being planted in your energy system. Each sound calls its associated chakra into expression. For anahata, the seed syllable is *Yam*, pronounced "yum" or "yahm."

Take a moment to sit quietly in a location where you will not feel self-conscious about being heard. Take a few deep, clearing breaths, consciously releasing as much tension as possible from your body. Sit up with a straight spine, opening your chest and throat. Warm up your vocal cords and diaphragm with deep sounds of *ah* (as in the word "odd") on your exhalations. Chant the sound with the power of the belly and feel it reverberating in the chest cavity. Repeat ten times.

Now set a timer for five to ten minutes. Bring your awareness to just behind your sternum. Breathe in deeply, and chant the sound of *Yam* the same way for the full length of the exhalation. As you continue, maintain the erect spine while softening the body as much as possible. Feel the vibration of this bija mantra in the sternum and radiating outward in all directions. Imagine the sound breaking up patterns of tension and fear built up around the heart chakra. Imagine the heart chakra expanding and finding new steadiness in the vibration of your voice. When your timer goes off, take a moment to notice how you feel. Let whatever you feel register in your experience.

The arms and hands are physical extensions of the heart chakra, so it can be very helpful to place the hands in prayer position with the thumbs against the sternum. You will create a positive loop back to the heart chakra as well as more easily feel the vibrations in your hands and chest.

After a few sessions of vocalizing the bija mantra out loud, try repeating the sound internally, without using your voice. You can use this bija mantra any time you want to invoke the power of your fourth chakra. It can be especially helpful when combined with any of the yoga postures in chapter 5.

PRACTICE

WORK WITH A TRADITIONAL MANTRA

While each chakra will respond to its bija mantra, traditional mantras will benefit you more broadly. There are many traditional mantras associated with the heart chakra, especially when chanted in the context of devotional practices. In fact, a whole system of yoga, called bhakti, is centered around these heart-opening devotions, especially communal kirtan singing.

In this practice, you'll chant a very popular Hindu mantra in three ways: audibly, just as you did before; beneath your breath or silently with mala beads; and by singing.

The mantra to try is as follows.

Om Namo Bhagavate Vasudevaya

(pronounced Om NAH-moh BHAG-uh-
VAH-tey VAH-sooh-DAY-vai-yuh*)*

Although its true spiritual power cannot be put neatly into English words, a rough, piece-by-piece translation of this mantra may be helpful for orienting to it.

Om is often called the "universal sound" or "primal sound." It represents the essence of ultimate reality, consciousness, and the entire universe. Om is chanted at the beginning of many mantras to invoke spiritual energy and connect with the Divine. *Namo* can be translated as "I bow down to" or "I offer my salutations to." It's an expression of respect and humility. *Bhagavate* is a term often used to refer to God or the Divine in a personal, loving, and reverential way, although it also signifies the Supreme Being as the source of all existence and the ultimate reality. Finally, *Vasudevaya* is a name for Krishna, a revered deity in Hinduism. By chanting or singing this mantra, you are calling to the loving aspects of the Divine—romantic love, the love of parents for their children, and supreme love, to name a few—associated with Krishna. This mantra has great history and meaning, and I encourage you to read about it.

First, just as before, you will chant audibly. Prepare as you did with the bija mantra practice. Then repeat the entirety of the first practice with *Om Namo Bhagavate Vasudevaya* as your mantra. Audible chanting like this is the foundation of mantra practices.

Next, practice japa mala, silently repeating or lightly whispering this mantra under your breath using a set of 108 prayer beads—known as a mala—to keep count. With your mala draped over your middle finger and starting at the large guru bead, use your thumb to cycle slowly through the beads, pulling them toward you. You will repeat the mantra once for each bead as they pass through your fingers. After a complete cycle, if you would like to continue, turn the mala around and count in the other direction as you should never cross the guru bead. This is a very meditative practice that will lead to greater ease with the next method.

Finally, sing *Om Namo Bhagavate Vasudevaya* to a melody of your choice—with an instrument if you play one. Choose an easy and uplifting melody. I have a good friend who uses the familiar "Ode to Joy" from Beethoven's Ninth Symphony for many mantras. Because the heart chakra seeks connection and harmony, singing with others makes this practice more joyous and effective. If you love the feeling of chanting, I encourage you to seek out local kirtan groups.

INTUITING A PERSONAL MANTRA

While it may not have the spiritual technology of an ancient language like Sanskrit, having a personal mantra can be deeply meaningful and useful. In this last practice, I will guide you to create one yourself that can become a touchpoint to call your heart chakra back into an open state. Just as a souvenir from traveling becomes a portal to great memories and expansive feelings, mantras intuited during times of healing, connection, and openness can become customized tools for stimulating anahata.

For this practice, you will generate words or phrases that are infused with the energy of your expanded heart chakra. To do so, search your past experiences for moments when your heart chakra was undoubtedly expressing. You might have felt your heart surge when engaged in your favorite hobby or at the birth of your child, on a great vacation, or just sitting around the dinner table with family.

Visualize one of these important moments and allow yourself to experience fully the feelings of love there. Soak in them. Then hold on to the experience and shift your focus to the evolving physical sensations around your heart chakra. Perhaps a heaviness begins yielding to lightness.

Perhaps you notice easier breathing, a bubbling and joyful yet grounded feeling, or a sense of rightness about it all. As much as you can, slow down and feel.

Now your experience is ripe for listening for simple phrases that will encapsulate this moment. It could be any sound or sounds, and only you will know. You are crafting your own medicine. Phrases like "Heart to heart," "Here we are," "Loving togetherness," and "Yes, yes" are some simple examples. What is important is that you allow a phrase to come through spontaneously that both feels right and that you just love to say, chant, or sing repeatedly.

SUMMARY

Mantras are powerful tools that can disrupt restrictive thought patterns, particularly those limiting the expression of the fourth chakra. Through the three practices presented here—chanting the bija mantra, chanting or singing a traditional Sanskrit mantra, and generating your own mantra—you now have some basic tools for directly influencing and activating your fourth chakra.

Having a healed and whole heart chakra will help you come out of your own energetic hiding so you can feel a more effortless connection to yourself and others. Despite your story or the stories you tell yourself, you can show up in the world with a bold and boundless heart.

12

COLORS AND SHAPES

GINA NICOLE

There are many fabulous, natural ways to activate and attune your heart chakra so you can enjoy a high-vibing life. Two of my favorite methods are using full-spectrum colors and shapes, and this chapter will show you how to take advantage of these methods to attune your heart chakra.

MY FOURTH CHAKRA JOURNEY

When I began studying with Cyndi many years ago, I had a profound aha moment when I learned that the fourth chakra activates from the ages of 4½ to 6½ years old. I had been working intensely in therapy, uncovering a sexual abuse experience from those years that I had forgotten.

This lightbulb moment helped me recognize that some of what I had learned from family and where I fit in "my pack" was a mixed bag, and it launched me on a journey of heart chakra healing.

You don't have to master healing arts to apply these concepts to your heart. You only have to listen to your body and heed the wisdom of the fourth chakra—and use love as an asset to do so.

WORKING WITH SHAPES

Although there are many shapes you can use for strong fourth chakra activation, three in particular are most helpful for supporting this chakra:

Infinity Sign

BENEFITS: As the element of the heart chakra is air, it's all about space, expansion, and feeling the infinite. Therefore, the infinity sign is an ideal symbol to activate in the heart chakra. It represents unconditional love enduring eternally, faith in source energy, and can also symbolize everlasting love for some individuals.

VISUALLY: The infinity symbol looks like a horizontal figure-eight—a continuous, unbroken loop, typically with two loops intertwining. Imagine this symbol at the heart center activating infinite love or limitless possibilities.

QUALITIES WHEN OVERUSED: Perfectionism, dualism.

Heart

> **BENEFITS**: Hearts are commonly used to describe aspects of the fourth chakra such as affection, emotion, and love. They are often used to represent the center of our emotions.

> **VISUALLY**: Picture a beautiful, bright, lit heart shape at your heart center or around something you would like to send more love to. The edges of the heart enable protection and nourishment in relationships. You can imagine them around any person, place, or thing to increase unconditional love and harmony.

> **QUALITIES WHEN OVERUSED**: Too trusting, giving too much.

Rose

> **BENEFITS**: Roses are associated with the heart chakra qualities of love, romance, beauty, and courage. They are also one of the highest-frequency flowers.

> **VISUALLY**: Picture a rose blooming at your heart space. The blossoming energy enables connection with nature's beauty and infuses your space with high-frequency love. You can imagine roses around any person, place, or thing to increase

their vibrational frequency. All flowers are connected to the fire element, which activates purification, transmutation, passion, and assertiveness.

QUALITIES WHEN OVERUSED: Too assertive, aggressive, desiring too much.

PRACTICE

ACTIVATE AIR USING A SHAPE

The element of the heart chakra is air. When working with heart chakra energy, it is helpful to infuse the air around you, and you can do so by activating the air you breathe. The goal is to move freely like air and fill the air with love.

Imagine bringing one of the above shapes to your heart center. Breathe in, feeling the breath push your tummy outward, and on the out-breath, send this shape from your heart and your breath into the air around you. When you do so, visualize or intend the outcome of your desire in your mind's eye. Simultaneously assert an affirmation in the present tense to actualize the intention, such as:

I am connected at high frequency.
I breathe in love everywhere I go.

You can explore different shapes and intentions, changing the affirmation above to fit your desire. For instance, employ a circle for boundaries or a rose for higher-frequency connections.

PRACTICE

USING SPIRALS
TO RELEASE TENSION

As the spiral is traditionally associated with the heart chakra, you can use this shape to activate your heart energy, releasing whatever feels stuck within. One way I do this is to imagine energy moving from my heart, down my arms, and into my hands and then draw spiral shapes in my journal. As I learned in my feng shui training, energy naturally moves from left to right, so I make spirals in that direction.

Employ an affirmation such as this one:

I am life force energy. I feel flow in the
sensual pleasures that life delivers.

You can interact with shapes in any way that feels right. Play in the symbolism and try different combinations to see their benefits.

FOUR COLORS FOR ENLIGHTENING YOUR HEART CHAKRA

I use four colors for fourth chakra activation, and only one is green. As you examine the applications of each color, pay attention to the various representations, meanings, and support it provides. The next section will give suggestions on how you can use a particular color to activate and attune your heart chakra.

Green

BENEFITS: Green is fresh and stimulates renewal. It is an ideal color to use when you want to create emotional or physical healing, release what is old or outdated, and recharge with natural energy.

QUALITIES WHEN OVERUSED: Lack of focus, inability to complete a project, overinvolvement with others' issues.

AFFIRMATION: Love revitalizes my perspectives and my natural energy.

Pink

BENEFITS: Pink encourages heart chakra sensations of unconditional love and acceptance. Pink is a combination of red (fire) and white (spiritual) energy and will grow your healing abilities in a nurturing way.

QUALITIES WHEN OVERUSED: Lack of self-confidence and trust in self.

AFFIRMATION: I feel the unconditional love this pink inspires. It helps me follow my heart's desires.

Gold

BENEFITS: This very courageous color promotes compassion and oneness and sparks us to lead from the heart. Gold is an empowering and protective color that inspires us to harmonize, move forward in care, and see the best in others.

QUALITIES WHEN OVERUSED: Too disciplined, overprotective.

AFFIRMATION: I release what is dense and old as I come into oneness with harmonizing gold.

Blue

BENEFITS: Though blue is not commonly linked to the fourth chakra, it's beneficial to imagine blue at the heart center when it's hard to communicate your heart's truth, especially in conversation with challenging people. Blue is a calming color and will bring peace to you and more love to your messaging.

QUALITIES WHEN OVERUSED: Emotionally sharing too much, trusting the wrong people with a message.

AFFIRMATION: I communicate from my heart what is true as I invoke the color blue.

WORKING WITH COLOR

I consistently discover joy and a sense of vastness in aligning the heart chakra with different colors. While the fourth chakra is often associated with green, the addition of pink, gold, and blue means that you'll have many options in your practice.

Here are some brief and simple ideas of how to employ color to boost your heart chakra:

» Select a heart chakra color palette. Think of your heart chakra as a canvas. Prepare for a colorful adventure with your mind's eye by grabbing a vibrant paintbox and then painting your heart chakra's space with greens, pinks, gold, and blues. Move the brush strokes left to right and simultaneously feel the expansion of your heart center. You can form specific images or emphasize one or more colors rather than others to produce the desired impact.

» Deepen resonance with words and color. Select the heart color that matches the mood you want to create and write an affirmation on paper with the correct colored pen. Do you yearn for harmony? Choose a gold pen and write something like "My heart hums with harmony." Hold the paper to your chest and see that beautiful gold energy circling around your heart.

» Garden in your heart. Picture a whimsical garden. It's bursting with colorful flowers, each symbolizing a unique emotion or aspect of your heart. Care for this garden, nurturing the emotional blooms as they flourish in vibrant splendor.

» Generate a heart kaleidoscope. Think of your heart chakra as a kaleidoscope of emotions and energies, each represented by the four major heart colors. Twist this kaleidoscope and watch as your heart's colors shift and blend. Then ask a question and turn the kaleidoscope again, seeing how the hues formulate an image in response.

» Eat your greens! Seek out lettuce, kale, and other beautiful green leafy vegetables. See the recipes in the final chapter of this book for ideas.

» Engage with the colors of your heart with a joyful spirit and consider embracing the entire spectrum of colors available in the rainbow— and beyond. Remember that color is energy, and energy is color. Your heart chakra is intricately connected with all the other chakras within your being. The unity of our shared human experience illustrates that each subtle energy particle exists within everything else, emphasizing the interconnection of our inner and outer worlds.

SUMMARY

The world is made of colors and shapes. In this chapter you've learned that your heart chakra—your home of connection, relationships, and healing abilities—responds beautifully to a variety of colors and several different shapes. Use your imagination, intuition, or decor (in clothing or home environment) to bliss out that heart chakra.

13

RECIPES

You can best serve your fourth chakra by incorporating a wide array of green foods into your diet. Understanding and caring for this chakra with diverse green foods can lead to profound emotional and spiritual growth. It can also significantly contribute to overall heart health. These nutrient-dense items may lower the risk of heart disease by reducing cholesterol levels, managing blood pressure, and supporting overall cardiovascular function. They are also abundant in antioxidants that combat inflammation, preventing damage to blood vessels and reducing the risk of heart-related complications.

I start my day with organic green tea and often complement it with avocado toast. So delicious! For me, eating green helps keep me serene. There are so many options for green-centric foods for each meal, some of which I will share here. Let's explore green foods and three of my fourth chakra recipes.

HEART-HEALTHY GREEN FOODS

Following is a partial list of some of the green foods that will bolster and balance the fourth chakra.

- » asparagus
- » avocado
- » broccoli
- » celery
- » chard
- » collard greens
- » cucumber
- » dandelion greens
- » green apples
- » green lentils
- » green tea
- » kale
- » kiwi
- » lime
- » mint
- » parsley

» peas

» spinach

» spirulina

» swiss chard

» zucchini

Remember, when deciding which foods to eat, flexibility and diversity are critical. Don't hesitate to expand your meal choices, try new foods and recipes, and be creative with your meals to maintain a healthy and vibrant heart chakra.

To help diversify your home menu options and energize your heart chakra, here are three of my delectable, healthy, plant-based fourth chakra recipes: one each for breakfast, lunch, and dinner. Of course, you can mix and match and make these recipes at any time.

I recommend choosing organic food whenever possible and washing your fruits and vegetables to avoid unwanted dirt, debris, bugs, and pesticides.

I hope you enjoy these plant-based recipes and find they help you connect with and nourish your fourth chakra. Feel free to adapt them as your creativity and palate dictate. May these recipes encourage you to explore and discover others that help you tune in to your body, your chakras, and your overall health and well-being.

Heartwarming Green Wake-Up Smoothie

SERVES 1

This sublime smoothie will make you feel like the sun is out on a cloudy day.

> 1 cup fresh pineapple (frozen will work
>   if fresh is unavailable)
> 1 cup fresh kale leaves
> 1 cup fresh spinach leaves
> 1 small avocado, peeled
> ½ frozen banana, peeled
> Juice of ¼ fresh lime
> 1 cup plant-based milk of choice
> 1 cup coconut water
> Ice cubes (if you're using frozen fruit, reduce
>   or eliminate the ice cubes based on the
>   desired consistency)
> 1 tablespoon maple syrup, if desired (optional
>   and to taste; can substitute another preferred
>   natural sweetener)

Peel and chop the pineapple, kale, spinach, and avocado and place them in a blender. Add the frozen banana, lime juice, and plant-based milk of choice. Add the ice cubes, if using, and the maple syrup, if using, to taste. Blend until smooth and serve cold.

Happy Heart Green Goddess Salad

SERVES 2

This creative salad is perfect for a light lunch. Quinoa is a complete protein, so this recipe provides this vital nutrient as well as the fats and carbohydrates needed for a balanced meal.

FOR THE SALAD

1 cup uncooked quinoa, rinsed

2 cups water or vegetable broth

1 cup diced cucumber

1 cup broccoli florets, chopped and lightly steamed

1 cup baby spinach leaves

1 ripe avocado, peeled and diced

½ cup green peas (fresh or frozen and thawed)

¼ cup chopped green onions

¼ cup chopped fresh parsley

¼ cup chopped fresh basil leaves

More herbs or pumpkin or sunflower seeds for garnish, if desired

To prepare the salad, combine the rinsed quinoa with the water or vegetable broth in a saucepan. Bring it to a boil over medium heat, then reduce to low heat, cover, and let it simmer for about 15 minutes or until the quinoa is cooked and the water is absorbed. Fluff the quinoa with a fork and let it cool to room temperature.

FOR THE GREEN GODDESS DRESSING

- ½ cup fresh spinach leaves
- ¼ cup fresh basil leaves
- ¼ cup fresh parsley leaves
- ¼ cup plain plant-based dairy-free yogurt
- 2 tablespoons lemon juice, from bottle or freshly squeezed
- 2 tablespoons apple cider vinegar
- 1 garlic clove, minced
- 2 tablespoons extra virgin olive oil
- Salt and pepper to taste

While the quinoa is cooling, you can make the dressing. In a blender or food processor, combine all the dressing ingredients. Blend until smooth and creamy, and adjust the seasonings to your preference.

You can now assemble the salad. In a large mixing bowl, combine the cooked quinoa with the remaining salad ingredients. Toss gently to mix.

Drizzle the dressing over the quinoa salad and toss to coat all the ingredients evenly with the creamy goodness.

Divide the salad into individual bowls or plates. For added crunch and nutrition, top with additional fresh herbs or a sprinkle of seeds, such as pumpkin or sunflower seeds.

Heart-Healthy Zucchini and Chickpea Stir-Fry

SERVES 2

FOR THE STIR-FRY

2 medium-sized zucchinis, sliced into half moons

1 green bell pepper, thinly sliced

1 15-ounce can chickpeas, drained and rinsed, or

1½ cups cooked chickpeas

1 cup cherry tomatoes, halved

1 cup baby spinach leaves

1 cup kale leaves

FOR THE SAUCE

3 cloves garlic, minced

1 tablespoon grated fresh ginger

2 tablespoons tamari or coconut aminos

1 tablespoon sesame oil (or any other cooking oil

of your choice, such as avocado oil)

1 tablespoon rice vinegar

1 tablespoon maple syrup (or your preferred sweetener)

OTHER

1 tablespoon sesame seeds, for garnish

Fresh cilantro or parsley leaves, for garnish

Cooked brown rice or quinoa for serving,

about 1 cup per person

Prep the zucchini, bell pepper, chickpeas, and tomatoes, and set them aside. Then prepare the savory and slightly sweet stir-fry sauce by whisking together in a small bowl the minced garlic, grated ginger, tamari, sesame oil, rice vinegar, and maple syrup.

Make the stir-fry by first heating a large skillet or wok over medium-high heat. Add a splash of water or a drizzle of oil to the pan. Once the pan is hot, add the sliced zucchini and green bell pepper and stir-fry for 3 to 4 minutes or until the vegetables start to soften. Add the chickpeas to the skillet or wok and stir-fry for another 2 minutes. Toss in the halved cherry tomatoes and continue stir-frying for 1 to 2 minutes.

Pour the prepared sauce over the vegetables and chickpeas, ensuring they are evenly coated. Add the baby spinach and kale leaves to the skillet and gently stir until the spinach wilts and everything is well combined.

Remove the skillet from the heat. Serve this heart-healthy stir-fry over cooked quinoa or brown rice. Garnish with sesame seeds and fresh cilantro or parsley leaves for added flavor and presentation.

Note: Seeking extra healing power for your heart chakra? Then add herbs and spices such as hawthorn berry, jasmine, rose, basil, chamomile, sage, marjoram, thyme, parsley, cilantro, cayenne, or lavender.

PART 2: SUSAN WEIS-BOHLEN

When we make food related to the fourth chakra, we are bonding our heart chakra with that food. The chakra of silent love then empowers the food, and its nourishment brings love into all the cells of our body.

In this section I will offer three recipes derived from Ayurveda, the 5,000-year-old system of consciousness-based medicine of India designed to create good health. I have been inventing and presenting Ayurvedic recipes for decades and am thrilled to be doing so in relation to your heart chakra.

THE FOURTH CHAKRA
AND YOUR VATA DOSHA

In Ayurveda the fourth chakra is closely related to the vata dosha. This is one of three doshas, which are combinations of elements that make up the physical and emotional constituents of an individual. Vata is also a time of year, which means that everyone—not only vata-type personalities—can benefit from these recipes at some point or another. Technically, the vata season lasts from fall until midwinter and is linked to the dry and cold, but vata food can assist you anytime you need love, warmth, and grounding.

Vata is chiefly linked to the air element, which creates a pathway from the heart chakra to the throat chakra. Strong emotions of love and trust, forgiveness and sadness, and joy and devotion flow upward from the heart to the throat, where we find the power to speak our truth.

When we follow a diet to balance vata dosha, the air and space inherent in vata create a natural flow, opening the passage from heart to throat. When we are clear in our hearts, we can be clear with our words. If the heart chakra is out of balance, we can be filled with anger, rage, jealousy, and conditional love.

A vata-balancing diet includes foods that are unctuous, grounding, and deeply nourishing. Vata-supportive foods like nuts, avocados, oily fish, and some red meats are densely caloric, with the calories coming from fat, protein, and healthy oils.

Promote good physical and emotional health by looking for heart-healthy foods from local farmers markets, health food stores, or your own garden, consuming food that reflects all the colors of the rainbow.

Approach the recipes and foods in this section with joy and gratitude. Allowing your senses to appreciate the food while buying, preparing, and consuming it will enhance the experience, and your body will more easily digest the meal.

You'll naturally assimilate the nutrients and more efficiently eliminate waste. Avoid eating or preparing food if you are feeling shame, guilt, or anger. It can disturb your chakras and your digestion. Wait until you have calmed down or feel better. Do a calming, heart-centering exercise from this book and then eat. I promise the food will taste better.

The stars in these recipes are green veggies and colorful fruits: heart healthy, nutritious, and tasty. One recipe features tuna, so it works for pescatarians and meat eaters.

Heart-Centered Breakfast Smoothie

SERVES 2

Ayurveda typically doesn't love smoothies because they are served cold. The belief is that cold food is hard to digest, especially for vata dosha, which runs cold and dry. To make this smoothie more heart and vata friendly, we'll use warm water as well as flax seed oil and avocado for grounding.

> 2 cups filtered water, heated to warm
> 1 small ripe avocado, skinned and sliced
> 8 fresh mint leaves or 1 teaspoon dried mint
>   or ½ teaspoon mint extract
> 1 small cucumber with the peel and seeds
> 1 teaspoon spirulina powder
> 2 celery stalks, chopped
> 1 green apple, cored and sliced
> ¼ cup raw, unsalted pumpkin seeds
> ½ ripe mango or an entire banana (for sweetness)
> 1 teaspoon flax seed oil

Pour the water into a blender, add the remaining ingredients, and blend. Drink right away or place in an airtight jar in the fridge. If you refrigerate it, bring it to room temperature before drinking or add more warm water. Drink it on an empty stomach, and don't eat again until you feel hungry.

Sweet Roasted Brussels Sprouts

SERVES 2 AS A SIDE DISH OR 1 FOR A MAIN MEAL

Brussels sprouts may just be the first superfood. They contain fiber, carbs, protein, and nutrients like vitamins C and K. They are also loaded with antioxidants such as beta-carotene and kaempferol, which can prevent premature aging and reverse oxidation in the cells. They are a great source of omega-3, good for brain and heart health. A single cup of Brussels sprouts—which is not hard to eat with this recipe—gives you 10 percent of your daily omega-3 needs.

A note of caution: if you take blood thinners, you might want to avoid this recipe, as vitamin K can interfere with that medicine.

 1 pound Brussels sprouts
 ¼ cup olive oil
 1 teaspoon sea salt
 ½ teaspoon black pepper
 2 to 4 tablespoons maple syrup

Preheat the oven to 375°F. Rinse the Brussels sprouts under cold water and remove any discolored leaves. Slice off any stems that remain. If the sprouts are large, cut them in halves or quarters. If they're small—the size of a small walnut—you can leave them whole. Pat dry or allow them to air dry before roasting.

Place the oil, salt, pepper, and sprouts in a mixing bowl. Toss or stir to coat the sprouts with the oil and seasonings. Pour them onto a baking sheet or sheets. You will want to leave space between the sprouts so that they roast well. Place them in the oven.

Check the sprouts after about 10 minutes. Remove them from the oven and stir or flip them to even out the cooking. Cook them for another 10 minutes, remove them again, and pour the maple syrup directly over the sprouts. Cook the sprouts for another 10 minutes or until they are tender when pierced with a fork.

This dish is great over brown rice or steamed quinoa and as a side to protein such as grilled tofu or baked fish.

Grilled Tuna Encrusted with Green Herbs

Serves 2

This dish incorporates fish, which supports heart health, and herbs, which have healing properties and taste delicious. In Ayurveda fish is considered a vata food, pacifying in nature and rich in protein and many other nutrients. With high levels of omega-3 fatty acids, tuna can reduce the levels of the not-so-healthy omega-6 fatty acids and LDL cholesterol that can build up in the arteries of the heart. Tuna can also reduce the risk of cardiovascular disease and heart attacks, and it's one of the best dietary sources of vitamin D. Tuna is also a great source of other vitamins and minerals, such as iron, vitamin B6, potassium, selenium, and iodine. It's super for your heart health and happiness.

2 yellowfin tuna steaks, about an inch thick
  (16 ounces total)
1 tablespoon chopped fresh parsley
2 teaspoons chopped fresh oregano
1 teaspoon thyme leaves
1 teaspoon chopped rosemary
1 scallion, white and green parts, finely chopped
2 tablespoons extra virgin olive oil
A pinch of sea salt
Fresh lime slices

Place the tuna steaks in a mixing bowl and add the parsley, oregano, thyme, rosemary, scallion, and oil. Mix well to coat the tuna. If you have time, cover the tuna and allow it to marinate in the refrigerator for 30 minutes. If not, you can cook it right away. Heat a grill, grill pan, or frying pan and add the tuna, pouring any extra herb oil mix on top.

Cook the steaks for 5 minutes on one side, flip them, and cook them for another 3 minutes. Be careful not to overcook—the steaks should be rare. Serve with a few slices of lime and a side of sweet roasted brussels sprouts.

These tuna steaks are delicious hot but can also be prepared ahead of time and served at room temperature.

These heart-healthy recipes will nurture you—body, mind, and soul. They are good for all body types, and you can prepare them any time, adding proteins to the vegan recipes to suit your lifestyle.

CONCLUSION

Anahata, the chakra of unstruck sound. By this point in your journey, I imagine this definition has grown in importance and intensity.

Which sounds, tones, notes, and hopes are traditionally and indescribably silent? The answers include just about everything we hold meaningful: love, relationships, grace, spirit, the way our breath hangs in the air in the cold, the touch of a child's plump hand on our face.

In this book you were invited to learn about your heart chakra. That is a short summarizing sentence, but the book is full of complexities. In part 1 you were accompanied by the teachers and scholars of history. As you learned, your fourth chakra governs imperative biological functions related to your cardiovascular system, breasts, and lungs, among others. As a cauldron of green energy, it enhances all things "silent love," including love itself. The center of our healing capacities, this chakra has been revered across time for its connections to various Hindu icons as well as to a particular seed carrier, element, and so much more.

In part 2 you were treated to several different approaches to your heart chakra to help you more fully expand into your heart-based powers. Think of how many amazing relationships you can now enjoy with your fourth chakra spirit allies and all the benefits you can gain with the featured vibrational remedies, recipes, yoga postures, meditations, sound techniques, and other supportive practices you have learned.

How might you continue to enjoy the wonderment of your silent love chakra? As you continue to pursue your fourth chakra adventures with love, the possibilities are endless.

ANTHONY J. W. BENSON serves as a creative business strategist, manager, coach, producer, and writer specializing in working with consciously awake authors, speakers, musicians, entrepreneurs, and small and large businesses. He has shared his expertise on numerous podcasts and radio and television shows. Anthony has led a mindful plant-based lifestyle for over 35 years.

ANTHONYJWBENSON.COM
INJOICREATIVE.COM

JO-ANNE BROWN is an intuitive, energy healer, and author who lives in central Queensland, Australia, with a background including engineering and bioresonance therapy. She helps highly sensitive people find meaning in their profound emotional experiences and release disharmonious patterns. She is featured in the internationally bestselling multi-author book *Intuitive: Speaking Her Truth*.

JOANNEINTUITIVE.COM

LINDSAY FAUNTLEROY is a licensed acupuncturist and founder of The Spirit Seed, a school that offers personal and professional development courses that are rooted in ancestral understandings of health, humanity, nature, and the cosmos. Lindsay is a certified instructor for the National Certification Commission for Acupuncture and Oriental Medicine (NCCAOM), as well as a facilitator of the Flower Essence Society's global practitioner certification program.

OCEANSANDDRIVERS.COM
THESPIRITSEED.ORG/INOURELEMENTBOOK

AMANDA HUGGINS is an anxiety and mindfulness coach, certified yoga instructor, podcast host, author, and speaker. Her signature "Scientific, Spiritual, Practical" approach has helped thousands achieve transformation in mind, body, and soul. Besides presenting online courses, Amanda offers guidance on her podcast, *Anxiety Talks with Amanda*, and has an online community of over a half million followers.

INSTAGRAM AND TIKTOK @ITSAMANDAHUGGINS
AMANDAHUGGINSCOACHING.COM

MARGARET ANN LEMBO is the author of *The Essential Guide to Crystals, Chakra Awakening, Animal Totems and the Gemstone Kingdom, The Essential Guide to Aromatherapy and Vibrational Healing, Angels and Gemstone Guardians Cards, Gemstone Guardians and Your Soul Purpose,* among other titles. She is an award-winning aromatherapist and the owner of The Crystal Garden, the conscious living store and center of the Palm Beaches.

MARGARETANNLEMBO.COM
THECRYSTALGARDEN.COM

GINA NICOLE is a feng shui consultant, subtle energy medicine practitioner, and the author of a deck of wisdom cards. She encourages empathic people to orient their minds, bodies, spirits, and homes to align with higher frequencies to make impeccably clear and intuitive decisions. She loves to travel and is devoted to bringing transformational light to the foster care system.

GINANICOLE.NET

BLAKE TEDDER is a yoga instructor, musician, and guide who helps people connect to life and health by holding sacred spaces with movement, ritual, sound, and song. He formerly hosted the internationally acclaimed *Full Lotus Kirtan Show* and a podcast with yoga legends Angela Farmer and Victor van Kooten. When not attending to his full-time work for a university climate and sustainability team, he hosts a weekly radio show exploring contemplative musical landscapes and writes his own music.

BLAKETEDDER.COM

AMELIA VOGLER is an energy medicine and grounding specialist, internationally respected teacher of energy medicine, spiritual coach, and meditation guide. She embeds essential energetic practices in her meditations and teachings to better humanity. Maintaining an international private practice, she has helped thousands of individuals transform through grounding practices, intuitive insight, and advanced energy medicine.

AMELIAVOGLER.COM
VOGLERINSTITUTE.COM

SUSAN WEIS-BOHLEN is certified in Ayurveda from the Chopra Center and has studied with Dr. Vasant Lad and Amadea Morningstar. She has also served on the National Ayurvedic Medical Association (NAMA) Board of Directors since 2018. A former bookstore owner, Susan is also the author of *Ayurveda Beginner's Guide: Essential Ayurvedic Principles and Practices to Balance and Heal Naturally* and *Seasonal Self-Care Rituals: Eat, Breathe, Move, and Sleep Better—According to Your Dosha*.

BREATHEAYURVEDA.COM

TO WRITE TO THE AUTHOR

If you wish to contact the author or would like more information about this book, please write to the author in care of Llewellyn Worldwide and we will forward your request. Both the author and the publisher appreciate hearing from you and learning of your enjoyment of this book and how it has helped you. Llewellyn Worldwide cannot guarantee that every letter written to the author can be answered, but all will be forwarded. Please write to:

Cyndi Dale
c/o Llewellyn Worldwide
2143 Wooddale Drive
Woodbury, MN 55125-2989

Please enclose a self-addressed stamped envelope for reply or $1.00 to cover costs. If outside the USA, enclose an international postal reply coupon.

• • • • • •

Many of Llewellyn's authors have websites with additional information and resources. For more information, please visit our website:

WWW.LLEWELLYN.COM